RELIGION AND VIOLENCE, RELIGION AND PEACE

RELIGION AND VIOLENCE, RELIGION AND PEACE

*Essays from the
Center for Christian-Jewish
Understanding Conference
in Auschwitz, Poland
May 1998*

Edited by

Joseph H. Ehrenkranz
and David L. Coppola

SACRED HEART UNIVERSITY PRESS
FAIRFIELD, CONNECTICUT

#45024379

Library of Congress Cataloging-in-Publication Data

Center for Christian-Jewish Understanding. Conference (1998: Oswiecim, Poland)
    Religion and violence, religion and peace: essays from the Center for Christian-Jewish Understanding Conference in Auschwitz, Poland, May 1998 / edited by Joseph H. Ehrenkranz and David L. Coppola.
        p. cm.
    Includes bibliographical references and index.
    ISBN 1-888112-05-0
    1. Violence—Religious aspects—Congresses. 2. Peace—Religious aspects—Congresses. I. Ehrenkranz, Joseph H., 1926- II. Coppola, David L., 1959- III. Title.

BL65.V55 C46 1998
291.1'7873—dc21   00-045757

CONTENTS

PREFACE

For the first time in two millennia, Jews and Christians have the opportunity to put aside their divisiveness and seek reconciliation and understanding. The Center for Christian-Jewish Understanding (CCJU) advocates a respect for the dignity of all people and celebrates the special relationship between Jews and Christians. As an academic and research division of Sacred Heart University, Fairfield, Connecticut, and founded upon the principles outlined in the 1965 Vatican II document, *Nostra Aetate*, the CCJU promotes forums for dialogue and study in order to advance greater knowledge, understanding, and harmony between religions. The Center is committed to advancing and publishing the insights of religious leaders, scholars, and educators as they contribute to the disciplines of theology, philosophy, history, ethics, aesthetics, and pedagogy. This book is an invaluable resource for students of theology, as well as religious leaders and other adults involved in religious education. Most of all, it is written for those who are unafraid to imagine a world without violence.

On May 18, 1998, scholars, rabbis, priests, bishops, Islamic leaders, cardinals, members of the press, and observers from twelve countries gathered to discuss the role that religion plays in cultivating peace or promoting violence. I invited these people of good will to gather for a three-day conference on "Religion and Violence, Religion and Peace." We met at the Center for Dialogue and Prayer, a short walk from the main gates of the infamous Auschwitz-Birkenau death camp, where an estimated 1.5 million people, mostly Jews, were killed amidst the horror of the Nazi regime during World War II.

Not surprisingly, some participants expressed their uneasiness about my choice of the site for the conference. Peace is probably close to the last thing that thoughts of the Nazi concentration camp Auschwitz evokes. I chose Auschwitz because it is a symbol of the international cemetery which the world will be reduced to if we do not find some way to live in peace with one another. My aim in this coming together of continents was to see how we could cooperate in eliminating the violent direction so much religious teaching takes. I wanted to establish that violence in the name of God cannot be justified.

Among the many people who responded to my invitation were Mr. Sefko Omerbasic, president of the Meshihat of the Islamic Community of Croatia; Bishop John Brown, Episcopal bishop emeritus from Cyprus; Archbishop Jeremiasz of the Macedonian Orthodox Church; Father Remi E. Hoekman, secretary of the Holy See's Commission for Religious Relations with the Jews; Cahal Cardinal Daly, the retired Catholic Primate of All Ireland; Franciszek Cardinal Macharski, the Archbishop of Krakow, Poland; and William Cardinal Keeler, the Archbishop of Baltimore, who chairs the U.S. Bishops' Committee on Catholic-Jewish Relations.

Of special importance to the Center for Christian-Jewish Understanding was the participation by five Orthodox rabbis. They were from Jerusalem, the West Bank Settlement of Efrat, Paris, New York and Connecticut. Orthodox rabbis have considered interfaith discussion of religious doctrine to be forbidden, due to practices in the Middle Ages when "disputations" between rabbis and priests frequently resulted in a beaten or dead rabbi. In 1964, Rabbi Joseph Soloveitchik, the revered Orthodox leader of Boston and my teacher, reiterated the interdiction in an article entitled "Confrontation," in which he discouraged any theological discussions between Jews and Christians as long as Christians treated Jews as either objects of conversion or somehow as inferior. I believe that my former teacher would agree with me that the time is right for honest and equal dialogue to begin.

The CCJU conference at Auschwitz represents the first time that I am aware of where a prominent group of Orthodox rabbis participated in an interfaith discussion of a theological nature. I knew I was on the right track when this historic event received strong support from the Vatican. Edward Idris Cardinal Cassidy, president of the Vatican's Commission for Religious Relations with the Jews, wrote to me and said, "His Holiness Pope John

Paul II expresses strong encouragement for your endeavors and a sincere wish that your work may contribute to bringing about lasting peace for the whole human family."

The Catholic Church has been actively working for decades to enter into a theological dialogue with the full range of Judaism. The Vatican II document *Nostra Aetate* called for the revision of all texts and teaching to remove all anti-Jewish bias and repudiated any teachings that held that the Jews killed Jesus. This was followed by numerous papal statements on anti-Semitism, the on-going validity of Judaism (no longer "superseded" by Christianity), the *Shoah*, and the Vatican's recognition of the State of Israel, which have all led up to this historic opportunity. From a Jewish viewpoint, it is hardly believable that the Catholic Church is still accused of indifference to Jewish concerns. More has been achieved in the last 30 years than in the previous 2000. We are living in exceptional times.

I agree with Dr. Anthony J. Cernera, President of Sacred Heart University, who began the conference by saying, "We have come together because we believe that our respective religious traditions can contribute to creating a world where there is greater justice and peace. . . . This conference provides us with the opportunity to search together for meaning and to enter into honest and humble reflection together, in the hope that we can—because we will work together—take a small step in the direction of fostering peace and overcoming violence."

The conference was a respectful, balanced, and cautious dialogue discussing peace and violence in religion. Those who attended heard papers on the roots of peace in the Torah, the New Testament, and the Qur'an. Speakers warned that religions still have the potential to incite wars and, as such, have a grave responsibility to foster a spirituality committed to preserving life and cultures of justice.

My good friend, Dr. Samuel Pisar, an international attorney from Paris and New York and a survivor of Auschwitz, described the violence that he, his family, and friends experienced. In his moving address entitled "Blood and Hope," he said, "On these killing fields, we dare not forget that the past can also be prologue. . . . Fundamentalism, fanaticism, all ideologies that despise the human being can push our societies toward a new delirium of violence."

The subject of fundamentalism and fanaticism in religion surfaced several times in the course of the conference. The most systematic presentation on the roots and causes of fundamentalism came from Dr. Martin Marty, Fairfax M. Cone Distinguished Service Professor at the University of Chicago. This world-renowned scholar and expert on religion and society discussed fundamentalism and how it can be a precursor to violence. The Muslim speakers at the conference stressed that the Qur'an outlaws violence and that the contemporary examples of violence committed in the name of religious *jihad* bore "no relation whatever" to authentic Islam.

In late afternoon of the second day, participants were invited to visit the Auschwitz-Birkenau Nazi death camp. This is, in the words of Dr. Pisar, "a cursed and sacred place," "the modern Golgotha." Standing on the site of a destroyed crematorium, the only possible response by the participants was prayer, sung and spoken in Hebrew, Arabic, English, and Spanish. All were drawn into the fundamental truth: we are all God's creation, all life is sacred. The next day, with the images of the death camp still fresh in our minds, many of us concurred that it had been impossible to sleep because the wailing sounds of the trains by the hotel echoed like the *Kaddish*, the Jewish prayers for the dead.

One does not expect monumental accomplishments at a three-day conference. However, it was clear that new friendships had been formed and trust had been strengthened through honest dialogue. His Eminence, Jeremiasz, Orthodox Archbishop of Wroclaw and Szczecin, Poland, said that this was the first time he had been at a meeting like this where people of different faiths could share ideas and break bread in peace. Cahal Cardinal Daly called the conference "an important step toward better interfaith relations. The Center for Christian-Jewish Understanding has come of age with this conference. It has extended its outreach into the various religious communities and become more convinced of the need to pursue its contacts with ever greater courage."

Rabbi David Rosen, executive director of the Anti-Defamation League in Israel, said in his closing remarks, "We therefore have to devote ourselves with renewed energy and vigor, because our work in gatherings like this is a testimony of what is possible. They are a sanctification of God's name. They are a testimony of divine presence in the world and of divine purpose in the world."

The Center for Christian-Jewish Understanding has now gathered the proceedings of the conference held in Auschwitz into this book, including two supplemental papers by Dr. David L. Coppola, director of conferences and publications for the CCJU, and Father Georges Cottier, O.P., Pope John Paul II's personal theologian. Dr. Coppola attended the conference, and his paper frames the issues and problems surrounding religion, peace, and violence, while Father Cottier's essay concludes the book by looking ahead to a future filled with scholarly cooperation and charitable dialogue between religions.

The conference did not end when we all left Auschwitz. On the contrary, the shared ideas and strengthened trust experienced at the conference continues in our friendships and through this book, which I hope will be read by many people in the pew. There is a fundamental link between religion and peace, and I believe that all genuine religious leaders are trying to bring their people toward a peaceful understanding of their faith. Religion must be the driving force that brings about peaceful existence on this planet. Political powers are often able to manipulate religious leaders to promote violence. By bringing together religious leaders of all three Abrahamic faiths, we now know that whether it is the Torah, the New Testament, or the Qur'an, all commandments evolving from these holy books point to the value of human life. As my friend, Rabbi Rene-Samuel Sirat, Chief Rabbi Emeritus of Europe, said so well: "There is no such thing as a holy war in Christianity, nor in Islam, nor in Judaism. Only peace is holy, for peace is the name of God."

A special word of thanks is due to my wife, Sandra, for her involvement in the daily preparation of special foods at the conference; Father Poitr Wrona, director of the Center for Prayer and Dialogue; Edward Piszek for his enthusiasm and support for this project and through whose office many of the details and arrangements in Poland were expedited; David L. Coppola, director of conferences and publications at the CCJU, for shaping this book and editing the papers; Berni Capozziello and Joan Jackson of the CCJU staff for their administrative support; Michelle Quinn and Christopher J. Sheehan for their editorial assistance; and Anthony J. Cernera and Sidney Gottlieb of the Sacred Heart University Press for their efforts in bringing this project to completion.

Rabbi Joseph H. Ehrenkranz
Executive Director
Center for Christian-Jewish Understanding
Sacred Heart University
Fairfield, Connecticut

ACKNOWLEDGMENTS

The conference, "Religion and Violence, Religion and Peace," held in Auschwitz-Birkenau, Poland, on May 18-20, 1998, was co-sponsored by the Center for Christian-Jewish Understanding of Sacred Heart University, Fairfield, Connecticut, and the Center for Dialogue and Prayer in Auschwitz, Poland, in association with Casa Argentina in Jerusalem; Inter-America, New York; and Interfaith International, Buenos Aires and Jerusalem; with the endorsement of the International Fellowship of Christians and Jews, Chicago; the Tanenbaum Center for Interreligious Understanding, New York; Three Faiths Forum, London; and the World Conference of Religion and Peace, New York.

The conference was also made possible in part by the generous support of the Jerome Belson Foundation, New York; B. L. Manager Foundation, Connecticut; the Castle Oil Corporation, New York; Mr. Edward Piszek, Pennsylvania; the Rich Foundation, Israel; Mr. and Mrs. Mauro C. Romita, New York; Mr. and Mrs. Joseph Roxe, Connecticut; Mr. and Mrs. Barry Sternlicht, Connecticut; and Mr. Stephen J. Sweeney, New York.

OPENING REMARKS

ANTHONY J. CERNERA

Opening Remarks

Good afternoon. Thank you very much for coming to this conference which has been in the works for a good number of years, a very early idea by Rabbi Joseph Ehrenkranz when we first began the Center for Christian-Jewish Understanding in 1992. This is an important meeting, and I believe that we have come together out of a deep desire to assist in creating a world where there will be greater understanding among all people. Furthermore, we have come together because we believe that our respective religious traditions can contribute to cultivating a world of greater justice and peace.

Sacred Heart University was founded in 1963 by Bishop Walter Curtis of the Diocese of Bridgeport in Connecticut. Bishop Curtis announced his intention to found the University in September of 1962, just before he left for the Second Vatican Council. His vision was to establish a university that would be run by lay people. When the University received an Apostolic Blessing from Pope Paul VI, the Holy Father called Sacred Heart University "a noble experiment in Catholic higher education."

The fact that the University was founded in the opening moments of the Second Vatican Council has marked the life of Sacred Heart University. We have sought to be faithful to the Second Vatican Council in our life as a university community, and therefore, it is wholly appropriate for this university to have among its important works a Center for Christian-Jewish Understanding.

When Rabbi Ehrenkranz and Rabbi Jack Bemporad expressed their willingness to dedicate themselves to the founding of this

Center for Christian-Jewish Understanding, we were ready to implement a very important new way of expressing what we believe our mission to be as a Catholic university in the modern world.

Why this conference? First, many of our societies are being battered by a rampant instrumental reason and by an excess of individualism. Where this is the case, there is an eclipse of concern about our goal of a just and compassionate society.

In his book *Who is Man*, Rabbi Abraham Heschel writes:

> One of the most frightening prospects we must face is that this earth may be populated by a race of beings which, though belonging to the race of *homo sapiens* according to biology, will be devoid of the qualities by which man is spiritually distinguished from the rest of organic creatures. To be human we must know what being human means, how to acquire it, and how to preserve it. (29)

Shortly before his death, E. F. Schumacher, the German-born British economist, said at a lecture: "After all, everything we do and talk about should be oriented toward and derived from an answer to the question: Why are we here in the world, anyhow?" Schumacher continues:

> We are not using the facilities the Creator has put at our disposal for the purpose of attaining our end. We do not even think about what our end is. We are using things only because they are there. Our engineers and our scientists produce something more we could use, so we must use it. We do things because it is possible to do them. We are a society that is rich in means and poor in purpose.

Second, it is my hope that our gathering will provide us with an opportunity to remind ourselves and those who will read the proceedings of this conference about the meaning and purpose of human life, and what our own traditions have to offer to understanding that meaning and purpose. We enter into these reflections on religion, violence, and peace in the full recognition that in the twentieth century we have seen massive brutality and destruction of human life.

Victor Frankl ends his book, *Man's Search for Meaning*, describing his experience at Auschwitz with these words: "A human being is not one thing among others; things determine each other. But man is ultimately self-determining. What he becomes within the limits of endowment and environment, he has made out of himself." Frankl continues:

> In the concentration camps, for example, in this living laboratory and on these testing grounds, we watched and witnessed some of our comrades behave like swine, while others behaved like saints. Man has both potentialities within himself. Which one is actualized depends on decisions, not on conditions. (212-13)

He then ends with this thought: "Our generation is realistic, for we have come to know what man is really all about. After all, man is that being who has invented the gas chambers of Auschwitz; however, he is also the being who has entered those chambers upright with the Lord's Prayer or the Shema Israel on his lips."

This conference provides us with the opportunity to search together for meaning and to enter into honest and humble reflection in the hope that we can—because we will work together—take a small step in the direction of fostering peace and overcoming violence.

Works Cited

Frankl, Victor. 1963. *Man's Search for Meaning.* New York: Pocket Books.
Heschel, Abraham. 1963. *Who Is Man?* Stanford: Stanford University Press.

Opening Remarks

M r. Chairman, ladies, and gentlemen, I wish to cordially greet all the participants of the conference on "Religion and Violence, Religion and Peace" sponsored by the Center for Christian-Jewish Understanding of Sacred Heart University in Fairfield, Connecticut, participants who represent the great monotheistic religions of Judaism, Christianity, and Islam.

Could there be anything in the world more precious and dear to humanity than religion which binds us to God, our Creator and Lord, which gives meaning to our lives? Only religion is able to offer us a comprehensive outlook on humanity and on reality. What was our origin? Where are we going? How should we live to gain our final goal of eternal life in God? Therefore, we should not be surprised that there were, and still are, people willing to give their lives for their religious beliefs. The history of the great monotheistic religions is marked by a commitment to the dignity of life and by the sacrifice of those who kept faith with God.

Unfortunately, one must ask and wonder how it was possible in the past and how it is possible now—though on a smaller scale than in the past—that people who believe in God, or who say they believe, could take the lives of believers of different religions or people representing different opinions, different visions of the world. That is why religion means intolerance for so many people. In fact, there are some people who think that religions are the main source of the conflicts and violence in today's world.

Such an opinion is not correct. The very spot where this conference is being held belies that opinion. We are at Auschwitz, where evil took place in unimaginable measures. Many hundreds of thousands of people were atrociously killed here. They were killed not by the hands of believing people. On the contrary, they were killed by those who considered themselves to be the masters of other people's lives and deaths.

Sincere authentic faith in God must be considered as an important factor for bringing peace among people, the best guarantee of peaceful, mutual relations between people. Religions unite people of all faiths who take deeply into their hearts God's commandment: "Thou shall not kill."

Standing in this place, it is impossible not to quote the words spoken here in Auschwitz nineteen years ago by Pope John II. The Holy Father pronounced these words commemorating the Auschwitz victims: "This inscription awakens the memory of the people whose sons and daughters were intended for total extermination. This people draws its origin from Abraham, our Father in faith, as was expressed by Paul of Tarsus. The very people who received from God the commandment, 'Thou shall not kill,' experienced in a special measure what is meant by killing. It is not permissible for anyone to pass by this inscription with indifference."

The three great monotheistic religions are in accord as to the image of God shown in the sacred books. The Hebrew Bible, the Christian Bible, and the Qur'an reveal that God is gracious and full of mercy and he desires life and peace, not death and violence. Should not humanity, made in God's image, imitate God and also bring peace and not do violence? To authentically follow God is to live in his peace, graciousness, and mercy.

Dear participants of this conference, I wish all of you fruitful deliberations marked by God's peaceful blessings.

Opening Remarks

In the Gospel according to Saint John, in the formal discourse, we read the following words of Jesus, "Peace I leave with you. My peace I give to you, but not as the world gives do I give to you" (John 14:27). These words of the Gospel point to the source of peace: it is Jesus Christ, the beloved Son of God. In the same formal discourse, we find the words which point to the way in which the peace of God is present among people. Jesus Christ says about himself that he is the Way, the Truth, and the Life.

The peace of God is present among people when they follow Jesus' example; Jesus is the Way when they act according to his teaching. The result of acting according to his teaching is the life. The life of a believer means accepting the whole New Testament. It should be distinctly stressed that the life about which Jesus speaks in John 14:6 has nothing to do with egoism. Jesus gives his own life to bestow life on all people and the whole world (John 3:16-17). To describe Jesus' attitude, Saint Paul uses the Greek term *kenosis*. In the Polish language we use similar words that mean renouncing oneself, self-rejecting, and humbling oneself. In English we hear the words, "He emptied and humbled himself" (Philippians 2:7-8). Jesus showed the truthfulness of those words by accepting death on the cross. The cross is the essence of Jesus Christ, and the Church's mission calls Christians to be willing to give their lives for others, even for the life of a person who is considered an enemy (Romans 5:10).

The central idea of peace in the New Testament finds its representation in the liturgical prayers of the Orthodox Church immediately after the most important moment of the eucharistic liturgy of Saint Basil the Great. The priest reads a prayer, during which he offers requests and petitions for the Church; those present in the church; the monks in deserts, mountains, and caves; the authorities; good and evil people; old and young people; the faint-hearted; those who surrendered to temptations; those possessed by demons and those who are forced into labor. Also among an Orthodox Christian's everyday prayers is one for those who hate us, harm us, or make mischief against us. We pray for them not to be lost to the Kingdom of God.

The peace about which Jesus Christ speaks is best understood in the context of the complete sacrifice of his life for all people and the whole world. Remembering this sacrifice, the essence of Jesus Christ's mission and teaching acquires a special meaning here at Auschwitz. This place becomes an examination of conscience challenging every Christian and every person. It is not sufficient to say that the Gulag was the product of an ideology which hated Christians, the Church, and Jesus Christ, although it is true that anti-Christian ideologies were based on the protests made by some Christians. It was a false and perverse "Christianity" that abused the motto "God is with us" and readily consecrated with prayers and holy water weapons meant to kill people from the other side of the front who were often people of the same faith. That counterfeit portrayal of Christianity forced many people, especially in the nineteenth and twentieth centuries, to protest. It often led to the negation of Christianity, or even to attempts at its total suppression.

We should stress here the facts. The building of the concentration camp at Auschwitz is a chain of violence directed against Christianity and every other form of faith in God. The extermination of millions of Jews in concentration camps and the mass destruction of Christian churches, especially Orthodox ones in the twentieth century, are the results of the same ideology.

Standing near the site of the concentration camp in Auschwitz, we seek the roots of peace found in the books of the New Testament, and we are compelled to ask many difficult and inconvenient questions. Historically speaking, Auschwitz was not designed and built by Christians. It was the product of an ideology which was hostile to Christianity and whose aim was to destroy it. The anti-Christian face of Nazism and other ideologies is now clearly visible. This does not mean, though, that Christians are without fault as far as Auschwitz is concerned; since they contributed to distortions of the Gospel and to ideas that made it possible for the ideologies which produced Auschwitz to come into being.

And so it must be asked, can we keep faith with God's covenant after Auschwitz? It is the same question which was asked many times by the prophets and the just ones of the Old Testament. It is not a new question. In the Epistle to the Hebrews, we hear the ominous words:

> For it is impossible to restore again to repentance those who have once been enlightened and have tasted the heavenly gift and have shared in the Holy Spirit and have tasted the goodness of the Word of God and powers of the age to come; and then have fallen away. Since, on their own, they are crucifying again the Son of God and are holding him up to contempt. For land which has drunk the rain that falls upon it repeatedly, produces a crop useful for those for whom it is cultivated, and receives a blessing from God. But if it produces thorns and thistles, it is worthless and on the verge of being cursed; its end is to be burnt. (Hebrews 6:4-8)

The pain contained in these words is very close to the pain—or maybe it is the same pain—which we hear in the words of the prophets of the Old Testament:

> Cross to the coast of Cyprus and look . . . examine with care. See if there has ever been such a thing as a nation which changed its gods, even though they are not gods. But my people have changed their glory for something that does not profit. . . . We appeal to the heavens for this. Be shocked, be utterly desolate, says the Lord, for my people have committed to evils; they have forsaken me, the fountain of living water, and hewed out cisterns for themselves, cracked cisterns that can hold no water. (Jeremiah 2:10-13)

The prophet Elijah also calls out in despair, "I have been very zealous for the Lord, the God of Hosts, for Israel has forsaken your covenant, thrown down your altars, and killed your prophets with the sword. I alone am left and they are seeking my life to take it away" (1 Kings, 19:14).

Sadly, Jews and Christians share the consequences of the violence of the twentieth century. Auschwitz, the Gulag, the devastated synagogues and churches are facts which haunt the experience and faith of contemporary Jews and Christians. We share a faithfulness to God, the Fathers, and a purity of faith that is beautiful. We should foster coalitions and draw strength from our deep spiritual kinship and our faithfulness to the one God.

In answer to the question of which commandment is the most important, Jesus cites Deuteronomy 6:4 and Leviticus 19:18:

> The first is, "Hear, O Israel, the Lord our God is Lord alone. You shall love the Lord your God with all your heart, with all your soul, with all your mind and with all your strength." The second is this, "You shall love your neighbor as yourself." There is not another commandment greater than this. (Mark 12:29-31)

A beautiful commentary on these words is found in the First Epistle of Saint John: "If someone says 'I love God' and hates his brother, he is a liar; for he who does not love his brother whom he has seen, how can he love God whom he has not seen?" (1 John 4:20).

In Jesus' teachings to his disciples, we find that the words which most frequently occur are peace and love. Peace and love are the key words of the New Testament. The history of the twentieth century shows their truth and the absolute necessity to live according to their essence. Where there is not enough love, peace is thwarted. The extermination camp at Auschwitz and all concentration camps in the whole history of the world are products of hate.

Finally, I would like to express my belief that the historical experience of humankind has clearly taught us one thing: No one who cares about peace will break God's commandment to love every human being.

PART I

The Problem of Violence

DAVID L. COPPOLA

The Problem of Religion, Violence, and Peace: An Uneasy Trilogy

> There is a season for everything, a time for
>   every occupation under heaven:
> A time for giving birth, a time for dying;
> A time for planting, a time for uprooting
>   what was planted.
> A time for killing, a time for healing;
> A time for tearing down, a time for building
>   up. . . .
> A time for war, a time for peace.
> > (Ecclesiastes 3)

Human beings have the power to do good or evil, to build up or tear down, to act peacefully or violently, to respect or oppress others. Drawing primarily on Jewish, Christian, and Islamic texts, as well as on philosophical and sociological concepts, I will examine religion and its relationship to violence from three distinct, but related perspectives; namely, that 1) religion is directly linked with violence; 2) religion functions as one among many factors that influence violence; and 3) religions are unwilling participants in the practice of violence. This essay begins by setting a context for the study of religion, violence, and peace, followed by a presentation of the three perspectives mentioned above, concluding with possibilities for the study and practice of future peace-making.

Overview

Human activity has smudged the glass of God's creation with violence. Wars continue to plague humanity. Military dictatorships, economic oppression, and cultural clashes have left our neighborhoods wounded by mob violence, murder, rape, theft, vandalism, and child abuse. The environment is seriously damaged by pollution and the irresponsible consumption of the earth's resources, and the unrestrained actions by industry, science, and technology have resulted in the extinction of innumerable species and threaten the survival of the human species in a nuclear conflagration.

Further, a culture of violence is manifesting itself increasingly in movies, sports, schools, relationships, on the highways, and in international conflicts. People turn on the television and cannot help but invite some form of violence into their living rooms. When people choose to view or sponsor violent shows or events, they open the doors of their hearts and homes to a culture of violence. The result: many people, young and old, when confronted with a challenge or obstacle, act out their frustrations through violent means.

The challenge in the next millennium is what the Catholic bishops of the United States championed in their pastoral letter aptly called *The Challenge of Peace*. This challenge can only be met with the power of wisdom, virtue, and mutual respect, as well as a commitment to understanding, dialogue, and compassion. Peace for the future will be adequately advanced only if religion is part of the process. It is religion that can reach into the depths of human struggles and the heights of human accomplishments to offer a balm to a wounded world.

Neither peace nor violence is a neutral enterprise. Both occur when people choose to build up or tear down. Peace is a promise of God but still involves human choice. Peace is a complex reality that requires the intergenerational and interreligious participation of individuals, institutions, and societies to seek the common good, based on justice and the dignity of the human person as a son or daughter of God. Peace is not merely the absence of war or the forced maintenance of a precarious balance of forces between enemies: peace is the choice by people of good will to cultivate a just society.

When a society is at peace, individuals have the potential to benefit from all the elements that promote a happy and fulfilled life: security, trust, freedom, justice, respect, tolerance, art, music, dance, drama, culture, meaningful work, leisure, cooperation, healthy relationships, covenantal living, law, and love. Most important, peace is the best condition for educating others about the values that demonstrate respect for human dignity, promote social solidarity, and allow for free moral choices to be made by individuals, families, communities, and societies. When violence unleashes the dogs of death, persons have little or no opportunity for choice or morality. Peace allows for a clarity, a clear vision of the common good, and is not obscured by anger, desire, or greed. Peace is founded upon God's love and becomes the fruit of love when people strive to achieve harmony and justice.

On the other hand, violence is not merely the natural state of entropy to be expected in the universe. A conventional definition describes violence as "physical force resulting in injury or destruction of property or persons in violation of general moral belief or civil law" (Edwards, 3). Violence is the worst expression of humanity's freedom of choice and is frequently the action of desperate, fearful, angry, ignorant, jealous, greedy or power-hungry people and societies. Violence inflicts the wounds of resentment, terror, and prejudice which fester into bitterness, revenge, and death. "Violence is hubris, fury, madness. There are no such things as major and minor violence" (Ellul, 99). Those who inflict violence or death on others assume the power over life and death. As such, violence is a display of idolatry. When people choose to act violently, they fail to acknowledge the value of life and fail to reverence the creation of God.

The more familiar one becomes with violence, the less violent it seems. The philosopher Paul Dumouchel notes, "Just as violence reduces the individual opponents to mirror-images of each other, so it destroys the differences that normally distinguish justice from revenge, arbitrator from opponent, and finally friend from foe" (13). In short, violence functions like a mirror and peace like a window. The former reflects back on the person in idolatry, and the latter opens out to a world waiting to be joined with others in the pursuits of justice and love.

Religion in the Pursuit of Peace

Religion is the result when people of faith in God or the gods participate in a system or set of beliefs, attitudes, and practices in a sustained way. Once a religion is established or institutionalized, that religion functions as a vehicle for the believers to remember God's deeds and revelations in the past and God's continued relationship with the group in the future through prayer, ritual, story, and communal celebrations.

Faith in God is the essential element that draws people together in a religious community, and the understanding and interpretation of that faith directly influences the violent or peaceful commitments and expressions of that religion. It has been said that if one has the faith of a mustard seed, he or she could move mountains (Matthew 17:20). Unfortunately, some people tend to see faith as a powerful sword, rather than a seed. One could ask whether such a sword-bearing faith is indeed faith or force. Religious faith should bring people together in peace. Faith, then, is closer to a journey or a relationship than to a fierce, coercing power of conviction to be right. No one was ever told in the Christian scriptures, for example, "Be healed, your *absolutely* correct answers have saved you." Faith is more about trusting God and becoming like small children, and not about being an army.

The root meaning of religion is "to bind." Religion seeks the ties that bind people of faith together in a common pursuit of worship, justice, art, morality, and a celebration and communication of culture. The gathering of a community of faith is an event that occurs in history, not in meta-history or myth. When a religion joins people together, the weaknesses of one member can be augmented by the strengths of others. When people commit themselves and join together in the name of God, they frequently become enthusiastic about spreading their message and mission.

Religion is a force that can foster unity and love. In contrast, science and technology cannot encompass adequately the entire truth of the beauty and mystery of human life. Ironically, the molecular structures at the foundation of scientific discovery and advancement, which are constantly changing and not visible to the naked eye, are perceived by many people to be more stable and reliable than religion. Religion is suspect because of its theological formulations based upon transcendent values and claims, as well as the erratic behaviors of some believers. The best expression of religious power binds and draws people together in social, legislative, and humanistic concerns, as well as charitable causes, respectful and scholarly sharing of spirituality and theology, and warm friendships. Admittedly, the past has been less than exemplary when religions have initiated, acquiesced to, or ignored the violence perpetrated in the name of God. Only integrity in relationships, demonstrated over time, can heal the misgivings and pain of the past. In this sense, religion is engaged in what the Jews call *tikkun olam*, the work of repairing the world, beginning with the world of religion.

When studying religion and violence, it would be unfair to compare the best examples of religion's ability to foster peace with the worst examples of society's failures at preserving peace and vice versa. The next section examines three ways that religion is directly linked with violence; namely, that a) religion has sought to experience transcendence with God by taking the life of humans or animals; b) religion may function as a dividing force between those who believe and those who do not believe; and c) religion appears to promote violence when some people affiliated with a religious group engage in or encourage such action.

Religion Directly Linked with Violence

Saint Augustine once wrote that the human heart "is restless until it rests" in God (43). The cornerstone and stumbling block of religion is the human desire to communicate and to be in relationship with the divine. It is this restlessness and desire for divine communion that can lead human beings down the path of violence or peace. When humans are not able to trust and rest in God, then religion has functioned as a vehicle to manufacture the power of awe, fear, and transcendence through violence and death.

A feeling of unity and commonality is shared by the witnesses of violence who are drawn into the experience and mistakenly equate that counterfeit experience with an authentic encounter with God.

Among human experiences, there is probably nothing more powerful than blood and death to invoke awe. Perhaps a dead human body is the most primitive sacred object. Heschel said, "In the presence of death there is only silence, and a sense of awe" (1969, 533). Girard commented, "In the end, the tomb is the first and only cultural symbol" (1987, 83). The experience and explanation of death is a fundamental concern of all religions. Socrates asserted that the unexamined life was not worth living, but he was also condemned to death by the polis by a vote of 280 to 220. It is probably true that the way a society examines or does not examine death reveals much of what that society believes about the value of life.

Religion was the primary vehicle by which ancient tribal societies and cultures engaged in analysis, interpretation, and synthesis of significant events. Most religions portrayed creation and the workings of the cosmos by telling violent myths that evoked fear and mystification. Through awe-inspiring rituals, which frequently culminated in sacrificial bloodletting, violent encounters, or scapegoating, notions like "sacred violence" for the sake of prayer, protection, revenge, or retribution were woven into the fabric of primitive cultures. These choreographed rituals were laced with myths to heighten the participants' encounter with the beyond while dulling their senses to the fact that violence and killing were about to occur. Worshipers who became warriors offered preparatory sacrifices in order to galvanize their courage and focus their resolve. The violence was intoxicating and contagious and could run out of control, as was perhaps the case in the deaths of Aaron's two sons, Nadab and Abihu, in Leviticus 10:1-3 (Bailie).

Scholars explain the phenomenon of sacrifice with interpretations ranging from a gift offered by individuals or the community to establish communion with God, to a communal meal, to rites of passage until the victim was released into the divine reality (sacrificed), to atonement, expiation, or propitiation for offenses (Williams). Durkheim asserted that sacrifices functioned as a way for believers both to commune with God and make an offering to God, whereby the ritual sacrifice served to reinforce the social order of the essential interdependence of the individual and society.

Girard (1979, 1986), on the other hand, viewed sacrifices not as expressions or metaphors of a theology or the social order, but as signs of the original violent actions taken against the scapegoated victims by the society. This original violence was then cloaked in the language of myth. Thus, the animal to be killed was portrayed in the ritual merely as an object or scapegoat, and the person to be sacrificed or the people to be attacked were reduced to "others," with their individual humanity obfuscated, while the attackers understood themselves to be participants in sacred violence. This human delusion continued the cycle of myth and violence, and served to conceal the original violent actions taken by the community against the victims.

The first recorded death in the Bible was not a sacrifice but rather, a murder—Cain slays his brother Abel (Genesis 4:8). God banishes Cain and marks him with the scar of his own violence—fratricide. It is significant to note that the mark of Cain is described in Genesis 4 as God's way of protecting him from being killed by others, not a brand of shame or death. This "protection" was apparently accomplished by intimidation, since anyone who saw Cain would know that he was from a clan that would exact blood for blood. Nevertheless, Cain's killing of his brother fills the earth with violence, a reality that became an unfortunate and repeated way of life and death for all humanity (Williams). "The earth was corrupt in God's sight, and the earth was filled with violence" (Genesis 6:11).

Although the murder of Abel highlights the competition between the shepherds and farmers which resulted in a kind of cultural and religious rivalry, the reader is told in Genesis 4 that God favored the animal sacrifices of Abel over the grain offerings of Cain. This is an important point because the writer of the Genesis account is convinced that blood sacrifices "work better" when seeking to command divine attention. The moving but near tragic story of Abraham and his son Isaac (Genesis 22) concludes with a slaughter of a ram caught in a bush as a burnt offering to

God. Child sacrifice is prevented, but sacrifice is still seen as an appropriate way to worship God.

The second way that religion is directly linked with violence is when it functions as a dividing force between believers and nonbelievers. It might seem obvious to many people that it is more important to love God than to spend most of the time defending all of the correct answers and perfect definitions of God to unbelievers. Such has not always been the case. Doctrines and dogmas draw lines in the sand, and defense of those formulas makes people dig battle lines wide and deep into the earth, separating people for centuries. Religions seek to teach the truth of God and how God has been revealed. The definition of truth, when presented in a dogmatic fashion and accompanied by forced adherence, sets up adversarial boundaries where the strong and powerful own, police, and enforce the truth in ways that lead to violence.

The experience of mystery and the interpretation of revelation occasionally lead people to take sides which contribute to the strengthening of other divisions along theological, philosophical, gender, class, ethnic, cultural, and geographical differences. Differences among people can be a source of inspiration and creativity, but social unity is frequently understood in terms of external control, uniformity or permanence, rather than stability, which would allow for an essential unity in diversity. When religion is overly concerned with uniformity, comparison, and competition, then envy and violence begin to seep into its soul. Unfortunately, human violence has been consistently directed toward those who are different or weak. For example, people with physical or mental disabilities or challenges were thought to bear the "mark" of divine violence and punishment. Thus, humans created God in their own image, making God a violent and vindictive force who was as unpredictable as the forces of nature.

On October 26, 1986, the World Day of Peace in Assisi, Italy, Pope John Paul II said, "Catholics have not always been peacemakers." This frank admission by a pope, which could have been spoken by the leaders of every religion about their own traditions, is the beginning of a process of honest self-reflection for the Catholic Church. Religious groups have frequently claimed that God was on their side, which is much different from the claim to seek to be on God's side. Of course, it is debatable whether God has, makes, or takes sides at all. Nonetheless, the making of sides is a common practice that religion has been unable to escape.

To ask followers to sacrifice and transcend their individual desires to serve a common goal, such as fighting in a war, requires a rationale that appeals to the common good. Religious transcendence requires time, preparation, prayer, discernment, and communal dialogue. Religion seeks to understand the existential and transcendental meaning of life. The most expedient and common way to evoke a spontaneous response from followers is by inciting rage or enacting violence. For violence to be directed outward, there must be an object, an "other," which requires a person or group to be on the other's side. The making of sides, then, galvanizes commitment from followers who are asked to participate in violence against the others. Thus, during the First Crusade, Pope Urban II told the crusaders that God wanted them to enact violence because God was on their side in war. Perhaps similar words have been spoken when religious leaders have gathered at the White House to pray for the successful bombing of another country.

A third way that religion is directly linked with violence is when people affiliated with a religious group consciously engage in or encourage such action. Of course, the Jim Jones and Waco, Texas, incidents illustrate the fact that many people involved in violent actions are not directly associated with religion at all. However, "religious wars," crusades, inquisitions, *jihads*, assassinations of religious and political leaders, fundamentalist revolutions, ethnic cleansings, and the bombing of abortion clinics and government buildings are all examples of violence that have been rationalized in the name of religion by people who have considered themselves to be religious. These events become even more difficult to interpret when the perpetrators of violence selectively use direct quotations from their scriptures to justify their actions, or use symbols inappropriately, as in the case of the KKK burning a cross as a calling card for fear and terror, rather than peace and forgiveness (Douglas).

To further complicate the fact that religious people engage in violent actions, some do so consciously and in accordance with the dictates of their conscience. For example, in the 1960s, despite the criticism of Dorothy Day and several political and religious leaders, people affiliated with several religious groups destroyed private property, burned draft cards, destroyed Selective Service files, and poured blood on people in order to achieve the result of extricating United States troops from Vietnam. Compared to the stunning images on international television of destroyed villages, dead children, and monks who incinerated themselves in protest of the Vietnam conflict, the burning of draft cards was significantly less violent. However, some proponents of "liberation theology" advocate considerable violence if the result is a resolution of unjust, oppressive, and intolerable conditions—provided that the foreseeable result is not worse than the unjust situation to be alleviated. Guzman summarizes this well:

> Violence is not excluded from the Christian ethic, because if Christianity is concerned with eliminating the serious evils which we suffer and saving us from the continuous violence in which we live without possible solution, the ethic is to be violent, once and for all, in order to destroy the violence which the economic minorities exercise against the people. (77)

This kind of theological ideology and course of action presents its own set of problems, especially when discerning "serious evils," hopeless oppression, and proportionate ends. Further, an over-emphasis on heaven or another life after this one may have the effect of devaluing the importance of this life, thereby justifying mass martyrdom or suicide and encouraging revolutions and so-called holy wars.

The map for the journey of peace begins with cartographers of faith seeking to identify the roots of violence. So far this essay has examined three ways that religion and people associated with religion have not always been peace makers. The next section examines how religion functions to promote violence. By discussing the four areas of a) human nature; b) the need for people to survive; c) the social construction of knowledge and ideas; and d) the relationship of religion with the institutional and legal actions of a society, a more adequate appraisal of the role of religion in promoting violence will surface, especially when religion is understood in relation to these other factors and realities of social life.

Religion as One of Many Factors that Promote Violence

Human Nature

The presence of so much violence around the globe is a clarion call to people of good will to awaken and face the spiritual, religious, and cultural crisis of the modern world. Religion is one among many factors that promote violence. One explanation for this propensity toward violence is a flawed or evil human nature. The famous fragment 80 by the Greek philosopher, Heraclitus, asserts that it is, indeed, violence that creates and destroys all things: "We must know that war is common to all and strife is justice, and that all things come into being and pass away through strife" (Copleston, 40). According to Heraclitus, then, all things, including humans and human societies, come into being and pass away through strife. In this view, humans are created in strife and are condemned to express themselves violently. Despite the fact that people act virtuously and wisely on occasion, human nature is essentially flawed and violent.

Some religions have offered another compelling description of human nature: humans are freely created by a loving God. In this view, humans are not the result of a strife-filled, chaotic conception, but are freely called by name as God's beloved sons and daughters to share in the divine image and God-given rights. Thus, when one looks at "the other," one looks into the eyes of God's beloved creation. Humans are good, even if they do bad things.

The discussion of a flawed human nature is complicated by the events of the twentieth century, which are unparalleled in their scope of atrocity, most notably, the dropping of the atomic bomb, chemical warfare, ethnic cleansing, terrorist attacks, and massive genocidal programs undertaken by totalitarian regimes.

The Nazis, for example, killed eleven million people, six million of whom were systematically killed because they were Jewish. Heschel called the *Shoah*, "the altar of Satan on which millions of human lives were exterminated to evil's greater glory" (1966). In the midst of these grim events, many people lost their lives standing up for what was righteous and just in the sight of God. Presumably, many evildoers lived privileged lives of comfort and security. The question of evil and the responses of theodicy give some indication of the complexity involved in understanding human nature in the context of divine intimacy and human inter-action. In short, if human nature is essentially flawed and prone to violence, then religions must commit themselves to cultivate virtue and justice or reap a harvest of violence and strife.

The Need for People to Survive

A second area to be considered when examining how religion functions as one among many factors that promote violence is the need for people to survive. The concept of survival is multidimensional and here is presented from five perspectives: biological sustenance, self-defense, cultural preservation, secure public space, and preserved sacred spaces.

All living things compete to survive. Animals compete, fight, and kill for dominance in the herd or group. Some of this fighting and violence is due to competition for the food supply or mating opportunities. As humans have evolved, we also have participated in this competition, but we now can choose to respond to conflicts and challenges in ways other than violence. A necessary component for biological survival is access to the land's resources. Land is necessary because it provides food, water, clothing, and shelter—all the elements required for basic biological survival. Religion has always been concerned with simple survival as well as with transcendental pursuits. Ancient religions advocated fertility rituals that ranged from benign dancing to the sacrifice of life in order to gain the attention of the gods for a successful hunt or a fruitful harvest. When threatened with starvation or death, people will obviously do what they can to survive. The need to protect the food and water supply and the competition with others for these sources of sustenance were ritualized by ancient religious practice to endow warriors with a sense of mission and duty towards the tribe or group. The land, as well as access to the goods or crops from that land, was essential for survival.

The commandment "Thou shall not covet" (Exodus 20:17) attempts to maintain social order and reduce violence as much as "Thou shall not kill" (Williams). The lawful competition for food and goods does not curb the realities of selfishness and greed, which are powerful motivations for many people. When combined with selfishness, greed always leads to taking from others violently. Despite Girard's theory of mimetic desire and the scapegoating mechanism as an explanation for violence (1979, 1986), it is still unclear why some people feel compelled to mar or destroy works of art through vandalism, graffiti, or the taking of a hammer to Michelangelo's *Pieta* in Rome, for example, or what causes some people to destroy or kill that which they cannot possess, as in the story of Susanna found in the Book of Daniel (chapter 13).

On March 26, 1967, Pope Paul VI issued the encyclical letter *Populorum Progressio* (*On the Development of Peoples*). In it, he offered an economic interpretation of the sources of war and argued for economic justice as the surest road to peace. He contended that when societies are unjust, inevitably the stage is set for violence. A structure of violence is built into societies that do not seriously address poverty, unemployment, oppression, disease, exclusion, discrimination, and non-access to technological or basic resources. When colonialism, capitalism, communism, or socialism are governed without a sense of justice or transcendent ethical values, then disparities, inequality of power, and violent popular reactions become more common, and cycles of violence become rooted in the identity of the people struggling to survive. Further, prestige, position, and power are all subtexts of violence. When a religion aspires to positions of power and prestige, it is not only sustaining the social order but also setting the context for violence and oppression.

A second kind of survival is the right to self-defense in order to preserve life and property. In addition to being a necessary biological component for survival, access to a secure land and its resources is also a necessary component for the security concerns of a state or nation which, in turn, preserves the life and property of individuals, groups, and religions. There is a tension between peace and the need for self-defense, especially when a society's legitimate right to security and justice for its people is threatened by lawlessness or war. In such an instance, the society has the duty to protect itself in the most reasonable and proportional manner possible. The Qur'an succinctly and rhetorically asks, "Will you not fight a folk who broke their solemn pledges and proposed to drive out the Prophet and did attack you first?" (9:13) Of course, the right to self-defense is a complex issue in the arena of international politics, and it is especially difficult to consider any kind of proportionate self-defense in the event of nuclear war.

Secure national borders would not be necessary if wars were eradicated, but such is not the case. Countries strengthen their borders and their identity by creating military and economic boundaries reinforced by cultural and religious differences. Religious people want to preserve their cultural and religious traditions and share them with future generations, and clearly they do not desire to be killed or destroyed. As such, religions do not impede the violence that seems necessary for the protection of human lives, values, and goods.

A third kind of survival is the self-determination and preservation of a nation's identity and culture (deVries and Weber). Human history has been a chronicle of violence where peoples have sought to establish their identity by fighting for their destiny. When a society or culture is threatened or falls apart, "invariably there is violence," that is, "every state is founded on violence and cannot maintain itself save by and through violence" (Ellul, 84). Violence has been disguised under the mantel of respectability and religion in order to settle the chaos and restore the social order. Violence has been the predominant way to solve internal and external problems and has been the primary way that culture has been founded.

Part of the process of forming a cultural identity is differentiation, whereby a group identifies itself as distinct and autonomous from others. But culture does not have a totalitarian character and is marked by the diversity, ambiguity, and selectivity of the people who comprise a society. However, the forming of social identity with a cultural cohesion is most unfortunate when religion surrenders to the state's claim for autonomy over and against "the others" in the decision to wield violence within and without its boundaries.

A culture's identity is also shaped by its history, as well as by the way it responds to contemporary challenges. In times of adversity or threat, religions have advocated the practice of certain types of violence to stop greater violence. In the midst of this reordering, a kind of sacred violence or sacred social violence is tacitly granted a moral preference by religion or official leaders to restore the social order to a tolerable place. As such, religion functions as a powerful part of the shaping of culture.

The writing of a country's history also becomes complex as Edwards controversially notes:

> When established states write and teach their history, they censor from it moral disapproval of the violence that was involved. Guilt and disapproval are transferred to the aboriginal people or the successive enemies of the state whose conquest has been necessary for the manifest destiny of the nation's power. So the writing of history in the various national communities, and even in the sectional subcommunities, consists largely in a chronicle of the glorious violence by which the frontier was expanded, dissident elements crushed, and foreign foes compelled to surrender. (116)

A fourth kind of survival is the preservation of public land or space necessary for relationships and social interaction. Without personal and communal space, people feel oppressed and lash out in violence. Public spaces in the forms of town halls, parks or preserves provide forums for citizens to celebrate the human spirit by participating in political, cultural, educational, and religious activities. The education of children, for example, can most efficiently be conducted in space that allows for focused work, as well as safe recreation. The access to and enjoyment of art by everyone also contributes to the survival and celebration of a culture. When art is stolen or destroyed, it is a loss for the entire community. Allocating space for others to meet socially, politically, spiritually, and creatively can build unity among diverse people through common pursuits, which is an important concern that religion also shares.

A fifth kind of survival for human culture is the preservation of sacred space and possessions by religions. "Human beings are invariably driven to ground their religious experience in the palpable reality of space" (Lane, 3). Further, there is an inherent social and spiritual "architecture of order" in space (Hamerton-Kelly, 3). Religions have justified the taking and protecting of land for the sake of religious survival and the preserving of the social order. Religions intend to preserve their art, assets, and buildings as well as ensure secure boundaries for their people. Churches, temples, mosques, synagogues, monasteries, and retreat centers are all deemed necessary for the spiritual and cultural growth of individuals and religions. If a religion is not permitted to build a temple or sacred space, it will either leave that area of fight for that space. Similarly, if a religious group owns property or buildings, it is not likely to give up that space without some resistance and would be inclined to encourage its followers to fight against unjust aggressors who might seek to destroy those places or steal those things that inspire people to pray. In the words of the Qur'an, "If God had not enabled people to defend themselves against one another, then all monasteries and churches and synagogues and mosques—in all of which God's name is abundantly extolled—all of them would have been destroyed" (22:40).

Taken together, these five perspectives of biological sustenance, self-defense, cultural preservation, secure public space, and preserved sacred spaces illuminate how religion can be an important influence in the survival of individuals, nations, cultures, and religious institutions, or as a tragic player in the drama of violence. The next section examines how religion functions as one among many factors that promote violence in the social construction of knowledge and ideas.

The Social Construction of Knowledge and Ideas

Power and dominance are sown in the field of culture, allowing violence to grow close to the surface of every society.

Violence can erupt at any time in the form of military coups, revolutions, robberies, riots in response to an unpopular jury verdict, or stampedes at rock concerts or soccer games. If a society is to survive, the members must measure, critique, and balance their participation in this culture of violence through honest self-reflection and clear articulation of their shared values and meanings.

Berger and Luckmann assert that subjective knowledge and meaning are socially constructed. In their view, "social order exists only as a product of human activity" (52). This human activity can be deliberate or unconscious. The self-understandings and meanings of a society are historically conditioned and communicated through the society's symbolic universe and are passed on through cultural structures, such as law, politics, education, language, rituals, and traditions.

In particular, religion is a part of the cultural meaning-making process in society. Religion communicates truth or mystery in ways that are appropriate to the listener's ability to hear and understand the message. Whenever a religion asserts something about God, it is also communicating something about its own self-understanding. The categories and language used to describe God are self-revealing. Bailie agrees with Girard (1979, 1987b) and asserts that religion, myth, philosophical ideas, and metaphors in poetry have *all* functioned to veil violence. He contends that true religion reveals and acts in history, whereas false religion conceals and hides behind the clouds of ambiguity and metaphors.

The philosopher Martin Heidegger noted that violence is inherent in the evolution of ideas. In a limited sense, individuals and societies "remake the world" (80), or at least their particular world, by providing the rational context or backdrop for events and interactions. Philosophical concepts, then, can illuminate the interpretation and understanding of historical events, or they can conceal the actual events in order to hide the reality of violence. Similarly, cultures prefer certain ideas because they have rejected others, depending upon how they wish to identify themselves. For example, Enlightenment thinkers, who disdained religion's propensity toward superstition and overly zealous religious passions among believers, sought to replace religion with rationalism. The rationalism and secularism of the Enlightenment allowed for many positive advances in society, notably, human rights and religious liberty. However, particularly after the Enlightenment there is also an underlying current of thought that blames religion as the major cause of all the violence in the world, and it appears to many that relativism is the only sensible belief in the modern academy, especially if one is to avoid the passion and potential violence of religion.

Unfortunately, Enlightenment thinking may have also paved the way for the rise of totalitarianism and nationalism. Countries attempt to manufacture the effects of religion through patriotism, power, prestige, and violence. Through violence, a country can be united by the social contagion of a common enemy, an "other," resulting in xenophobia, fatalism, war and valor categories, and violence-bonding. Ironically, extreme nationalism can isolate people from the common good. The idolatry of the state has a predilection for violence against individuals and outsiders. The neo-paganism of Nazi Germany that crested during World War II, coupled with an underlying anti-Judaism in Europe, was an infamous example of such idolatry and violence.

Excessive individualism also has a predilection for violence. Especially when coupled with capitalism, excessive individualism advocates individual profit as the primary motive, competition as the ultimate law, and private ownership in production without limits or social responsibility—all profound challenges to the common good and communal religious values. Money becomes the measure of morality in this social schema, and individuals can be reduced to objects that merely produce or trade capital.

In addition to nationalism and excessive individualism, the social phenomenon of fundamentalism can also become the fuel for violence when people flare up in response to a pluralistic, ambiguous, modern world. Whereas nationalism creates the notion of "outsiders," that is, the people who do not belong inside the borders of the country, and excessive individualism alienates the "self" from the common good, fundamentalism identifies the "other," who is different and combats those individuals, groups, or social trends that are perceived to be a threat to the law and order of the society. By socially constructing the language and reality of "outsiders," "self," and "others" through actions such as stereotyping, typifying, scapegoating, oversimplifying the enemy, advocating prejudice and extreme competition, inciting anger, and dismissing tolerance, groups and governments have a negative impact on others. When these groups or social movements use the language of religion or are supported by religion, the result can be terribly powerful and violent.

A final area to be considered when examining how religion functions as one among many factors that promote violence is the relationship of religion with the institutional and legal actions of a society.

Institutional Actions and Laws

Cultures and societies express who they are by what they say and do through their institutions. Religion is an important voice in the moral and cultural discourse of a society. Religions have a right and duty to form consciences, shape public values, and contribute to the moral consensus of the citizenry. As the perception of religion has gradually become secularized, the law is no longer able to justify its actions on religious grounds or with religious principles. Nonetheless, the arena that strongly holds most people's attention, at least in the constitutional governments of the West, is the justice system. Newspaper headlines, feature magazine articles, and television shows frequently portray disputes that are settled through the courts.

Religions attempt to safeguard against laws that go against the best insights and practices of human morality because the law is a primary carrier of culture. Therefore, the deliberations and considerations of law and faith are compatible. Both seek to work for a society of justice. One difficulty, however, is the contradictory ways that a society determines what is acceptable violence. Through its laws and customs, "institutional violence is given legitimacy within the society's rules of conflict" (Edwards, 7). West aptly notes:

> Violence is harm done to another outside the rules of
> conflict which such a society sets up. It may even be the

redress of grievances by means which society does not permit. For example, the occupation of a building by sit-in protesters may be regarded as violence, but not the planned eviction of the tenants from their homes at the expiration of their leases so that the landlord can tear down the buildings for his profit. Again, if the government of a poor country confiscates without compensation a foreign-owned business, its actions may be called violent, while the owner's systematic retention of the disproportionate profit from his enterprise, which led to the action, will not be so labeled. (14-15)

Both law and religion are threatened by any group that might glorify illegal violence, unreflective pragmatism, selfish hoarding of wealth, or a philosophy of disposableness where life and things are used up and thrown away. Such cultural excesses could tempt individuals and companies to use the law to hurt or oppress people in order to protect investments and contracts, rather than for the pursuit of justice and attainment of reasonable, humanitarian goals and values. Such cultural practices could find it pragmatic and legal to terminate the life of a fetus, eliminate a business competitor, or kill an unproductive elderly person. The philosopher Thomas Aquinas aptly warns in the *Summa Theologica*, "But insofar as it deviates from right reason, it is called an unjust law, and has the nature, not of law, but of violence" (633).

The Code of Hammurabi and the *Lex Talionis* were both attempts to limit violence from escalating into unchecked ethnic passions, hatreds, and blood feuds. During the Cold War of the later part of the twentieth century, where nations promoted a tyranny of fear in stockpiling weapons, the Mutual Assured Destruction Theory (MADT) promised equal results for any country that foolishly dared to initiate a nuclear war. This absurd equality was founded on fear. In daily life, however, individuals who desire to exact justice in the form of revenge might actually have the effect of perpetuating violence rather than limiting it.

The scapegoat ritual described in Leviticus 16 requires the high priest to annually send out a goat into the desert to die as an atonement for sin. This atonement theology was present in the words of Caiaphas, "It is better that one man should die for the people than for the whole nation to be destroyed" (John 11:50), and has a haunting echo in modern societies that advocate capital punishment as a legal form of vengeance. Consider, for example, the actions of hundreds of people observed at a tailgating party, celebrating the 1989 execution of Ted Bundy in Florida. Capital punishment does not seem to deter crime at all. If anything, capital punishment deludes the public into a false sense of security and robs them of a true appreciation of the sanctity of life with a sacrificial killing. Further, its dark ritual process too closely resembles ancient bloodletting sacrifices to appease the masses. Violence too often begets further violence, as observed in the "mob justice" of American lynchings, where the victims were often photographed, shot, mutilated, or burned—long after they had died (Raper; Tolnay and Beck).

McKenna rightly observes that the legal system has a "primitive liturgical imperative" (85). An eye for an eye and a tooth for a tooth was meant to be a custom that limited violence and encouraged generosity, not one that demanded and required exact retribution. When it is presumed that someone *must* pay for unfortunate events or even accidents, then the cycle of violence or misfortune continues (Girard, 1986; Schwager). Societies that advocate capital punishment risk imprisoning their own souls in the violence of death row. Retribution and forgiveness are institutional actions inherent in the law and act as boundaries that identify a society and culture. To the extent that religion has advocated revenge and strict justice, rather than forgiveness and mercy, then it has contributed to the violence that vigilantes have exacted on others in revenge, as well as beatings, torture, or capital punishment incurred by prisoners around the world.

By discussing the four topics of human nature—the need for people to survive, the social construction of knowledge and ideas, and the relationship of religion with the institutional and legal actions of a society—this essay has presented the complex role that religion plays in promoting violence in relation to the other factors and realities of social life. A final piece in this presentation briefly examines how religions are unwilling participants in the practice of violence.

Religion as an Unwilling Participant in Violence

A final aspect of the problem of religion and violence is when religions, as part of a society, are forced to participate in actions that the religions find reprehensible. It is clear that the best of all religions call for love, harmony, forgiveness, justice, and peace. The best of society would also claim the same. Pope Paul VI said:

> The Church cannot accept violence, especially the force of arms . . . because she knows that violence always provokes violence, and irresistibly engenders new forms of oppression and enslavement, which are often harder to bear than those from which they claimed to bring freedom. (*Evangelii Nuntiandi*, n. 37)

Most religious leaders would agree with the pontiff's analysis. Yet, because of circumstances beyond their knowledge or control, or because of the "force of habit" to issue "mechanical blessings" in the name of patriotism (Merton, 187), all religions have been unwilling and at times, unconscious participants in the history of violence.

First, politicians and those with ideological or nationalist agendas, who whitewash their violence in valor and holy war ideology, have exploited religion. Many well-intentioned people and religious groups have been manipulated by those more clever and powerful than they. Also, exaggerated fears and prejudices strongly influence the way that people act in life. Ignorance, pain, suspicion, prejudice, lack of security, and loss of faith or hope can all stoke the flames of violence. Despite the fact that religious people can no longer deny that all humans are ethically and anthropologically bound together, some governments willfully oppress, dehumanize, and demonize others in order to tie together a social unity with the thin threads of fear and insecurity. These governments would have their citizens believe that God is a patron of military victories and favors the powerful, the wealthy, and those who are brave enough to be violent. Such notions are seriously challenged by the examples of Job, the Suffering Servant found in Isaiah 53:7-8, the crucified Jesus, or the teachings of

Buddha (Girard, 1987a). Nonetheless, religious institutions reside in countries whose leaders choose war and violence. When these institutions are powerless to protest, then they must make a choice for the greatest possible good.

Second, the vast majority of Jewish, Christian, and Islamic scriptural verses concern themselves with following the will of God through the pursuits of justice, wisdom, peace, and love. However, there are also sufficient instances where the texts advocate violence (Schwager). Also, there is enough ambiguity in the metaphors of some religious texts to warrant a selective or partisan reading that could justify violence. When certain religious texts are used out of context to suit a contemporary political or ideological agenda, then religions have unwillingly aided these unethical and violent activities. The violence in Ireland, apartheid in South Africa, the KKK in the United States, ethnic cleansings, and mafia terrorisms are all shrouded in religious overtones that have nothing to do with the authentic expressions of religion. The solution is not to change the scriptural texts or to rewrite them. Rather, one task of religious leaders is to consciously teach and preach the scriptures in their entire context and moral framework, thus deterring an oversimplified and impatient interpretation that could lead to violence.

Third, religious leaders and religious people are not perfect. The desire to be holy and close to God causes some people to express themselves in purist, fundamentalist, and overly-pious ways. New pilgrims on the path of holiness, frequently excited and insecure about their new-found faith, sometimes may not be able to tolerate others who are following different paths. Also, some religious leaders and religious people abuse the trust placed in them by their people. They use their position for their own benefit and at the expense of others. These violations and abuses leave psychological, spiritual, and even physical scars on their victims. When the noble ideals of religious institutions are compromised by the actions of weak individuals, then religion unwillingly contributes to violence.

This essay suggested some ways that religion is one among many factors influencing violence, and an unwilling participant in the practice of violence. Taken together, these three perspectives point to the complex, multidimensional, and sensitive relationship between religion and violence. The conclusion of this paper offers some possibilities for future peace-making.

Moving Beyond: Possibilities for Future Peace-Making

The challenge of peace for religion is to ask how, not whether, violence can be stopped. We have never lacked for voices to proclaim peace and nonviolence. The voices of such people as Ghandi, Martin Luther King, Jr., and the Dali Lama remind us that peace-making is laboriously slow and requires personal sacrifices. Pope John Paul II said in a homily in 1982, "Like a cathedral, peace must be constructed patiently and with unshakable faith." To work for peace, three things must happen: we must move beyond apologies, beyond ideology, and beyond talking.

Beyond Apologies

All countries and religions have at some time participated directly or indirectly in violence. The first step towards peace is an honest appraisal and apology by people of good will. But the apology cannot be for the sake of political correctness; it must be offered with the sincere desire to repent and begin a new relationship. Religious people must challenge each other to apologize out of love's motivation and move beyond that apology to a relationship of justice and respect.

The human community cannot forget the past mistakes of religion, but neither can the past events prevent the work of peace in the future. The historical memory of pain and hurt cannot be removed by rational arguments alone. Only a gradual building of trust and understanding through relationships and friendships will allow healing and progress to occur. Moving beyond apologies to a *teshuva*—an act of repentance and renewal of relationships— means a conscious effort to work for healing and forgiveness. Revenge in the form of violence will always breed more violence. Moving beyond apologies will allow people of faith to sow seeds of peace, faith, respect, and responsibility, instead of continuously looking for the stones of accusation to hurl at each other.

Moving beyond apologies also means acknowledging that God is a part of our longings, involved in human history, and offers no religious justification for violence. God witnesses everything and trusts us to be people of courage and honesty who work for peace. All people are made in God's image and have dignity. The victims of war are people, members of families, members of God's family. True justice requires mercy, love, and nonviolence, because God loves all people and lets the sun shine and the rain fall on the just and the unjust.

Religion can offer opportunities to celebrate genuine humanity, perennial meaning, community, ritual, commitment to social justice, and education in virtuous living without violence.

Beyond Ideology

Of course, to speak of moving beyond ideology is an ideological position itself. This section is more concerned with not being stubbornly wedded to thought forms or ideologies that impede the path of peace. The Vatican II document *Gaudium et Spes* (1965) draws on the wisdom of Saint Augustine and Pope John XXIII, and offers an insightful instruction in this regard: "Let there be unity in what is necessary, freedom in what is doubtful, and charity in everything" (n. 92).

Moving beyond ideology means that people of good will must courageously face the oppressors of the past head on and not reduce them to objects, movements, or social trends, but rather consider them as people who acted badly. Forgiveness is one key to freedom from the dehumanizing shackles of hate and revenge. If people move beyond ideology, then they will also move out of the pit where they are primarily identified as "victims." This stigma robs them of their sense of worth and dignity, and breeds a psychology of entitlement without moral responsibility.

Life is more than ideas and abstract faith constructs. Engagement in life is moving beyond ideas to communal living, beyond formulas of belief to secure trust and faith. Imagination, intelligence, and discernment are necessary in order to strive for a culture beyond violence, where nonviolent conflict resolution, education for justice, dialogue, openness, prayer, reverence, respect for life, service, art, music, dance, and cultural celebrations all teach about others in the context of human dignity and the common good.

Moving beyond ideologies towards tolerance and respect is to choose to walk on a powerful path that leads to sustained peace. The notion of tolerance is predicated upon a choice-based conception of social life, and faces its challenges of instrumental bonds, cultural avoidance, and loss of sustained engagement in community. However, tolerance is a necessary foundation for the building up of respect and harmony among all people.

There is more than one path to the same God, and the ties that join are stronger than those forces which separate. In Islam, for example, the Qur'an says that God intends the existence of different religious communities on earth (49:13, 30:22) and that they must respect each other (49:11). However, the work of peace-making must also honestly challenge "all ethnic and nationalist claims, whether made in the name of Christianity, or Judaism, or Islam, or self-determination, or ethnic pride, or patriotism, or whatever other ideology is made to serve as a veil for violence" (Hamerton-Kelly, 3).

The work of peace does not weaken a nation's will but is concerned with preserving its soul (USCC, n. 304). Moving beyond ideology means that religious people can no longer uncritically observe the signs of the times without realizing that they are participating in a morally significant way. Once a person witnesses violence in the tear-filled and bloody faces of innocent children and adults, there is no returning to the pretense that violence does not injure the entire human family and is a necessary evil.

Conflict prevention is necessary for lasting peace and security, but it is only the beginning. The poet Robert Frost observed:

> Something there is that doesn't love a wall. . . .
> Before I built a wall I'd ask to know
> What I was walling in or walling out,
> And to whom I was like to give offense. . . .
> He will not go behind his father's saying,
> And he likes having thought of it so well
> He says again, "Good fences make good neighbors."

Strongly fortified boundaries and armed forces may restrain violence for a time but cannot root out enmity or force authentic reconciliation. Moving beyond ideology means that countries choose to beat their swords into plowshares (Isaiah 2:4) and share the bread of their labor with everyone on the planet. After all, the goods of the earth were originally given by God for the benefit of all people.

John XXIII, in *Pacem in Terris*, also offered guidelines for authentic peace beyond ideology. He asserted that every human has certain rights which flow with the common good. Some of these include a right to life and a worthy standard of living (n. 11); a right to moral and cultural values, such as respect, reputation, freedom to search the truth, express opinions, pursue art, and be informed truthfully about public events (n. 12); the right to worship according to one's conscience (n. 14); the right to freely choose one's state of life and education (n. 15); the right to health, fair treatment of women and children, workers' rights, the social duty inherent in the right of private property (nn. 18-22); the right to meetings and associations (n. 23); the right to emigrate and immigrate (n. 25); and the right to participate in the political process (n. 26). For true peace to be realized, John XXIII said that all states and countries must be treated with equal dignity (n. 86) and human society needs to be ordered toward the spiritual and must seek truth, knowledge, spiritual values, pleasure from the beautiful, and pass on a rich cultural heritage (n. 36).

Beyond Talking

A Machiavellian conception of power and violence is losing its ability to re-found culture as the roots of violence are laid bare. Religion must explore nonviolent methods of maintaining peace and resolving conflict (Merton; Sharp). Cooperation, respect, and dialogue can be the new foundations for the future of moral and peaceful action. Religions and religious people have a moral obligation to future generations to formulate behavioral guidelines with a broad, future-oriented perspective.

The common good and peace will be more nearly realized when people are treated with dignity and respect, and unjust, oppressive economic, gender, religious, and racial structures are dissolved. This will provide the necessary common ground for the common good to become a peaceful reality. This requires a moral conversion, a change of heart (Jeremiah 32:39), which will then change the culture. A peaceful culture presumes civil discourse, genuine dialogue, openness, respect, and the sharing of power and resources for the common good. Peace and justice take time. Personal morality requires reflection, dialogue, and action.

Common human experiences, such as confusion, anger, suffering, dishonesty, temptation, weakness, hunger, or illness, are opportunities for people to be drawn together and respond with love, forgiveness, support, and healing through prayer. A shared insight or understanding of individual religious traditions will shed light on all human spirituality and longing. Unity can be found in the rich diversity that God has chosen to reveal to all religions.

It is true that people will continue to die, and life and property will continue to be destroyed through violence, but that violence does not have to be committed in the name of God. God is the God of creation, not violence. God created all living things, and religious people who seek peace will find in the care of the earth a worthy and religious action for the preservation and passing on of all God's gifts to future generations. The glass of creation, though fingerprinted by our violence, still has the true ring of excellent crystal when raised in peace.

Works Cited

Aquinas, Saint Thomas. 1948. *Introduction to Saint Thomas Aquinas.* Ed. Austin C. Pegis. New York: Modern Library.

Augustine, *The Confessions of Saint Augustine.* 1960. Trans. John K. Ryan. New York: Image Books.

Bailie, Gil. 1997. *Violence Unveiled: Humanity at the Crossroads.* New York: Crossroad.

Berger, Peter, and Thomas Luckmann. 1967. *The Social Construction of Reality.* Garden City: Doubleday.

Copleston, Frederick. 1955. *A History of Philosophy: Volume I: Greece and Rome.* Westminster, MD: Newman.

deVries, Hent, and Samuel Weber, eds. 1997. *Violence, Identity, and Self-Determination*. Stanford: Stanford University Press.

Douglas, James W. 1968. *The Nonviolent Cross: A Theology of Revolution and Peace*. New York: Macmillan.

Dumouchel, Paul, ed. 1988. *Violence and Truth*. Stanford: Stanford University Press.

Durkheim, Emile. 1965. *The Elementary Forms of Religious Life*. Trans. John W. Swain. New York: Free Press.

Edwards, George R. 1972. *Jesus and the Politics of Violence*. New York: Harper & Row.

Ellul, Jacques. 1969. *Violence: Reflections from a Christian Perspective*. Trans. C. G. Kings. New York: Seabury.

Frost, Robert. 1979. "Mending Wall." In *The Norton Anthology of American Literature*. New York: W. W. Norton. (originally published in 1914)

Gaudium et Spes [*Pastoral Constitution on the Church in the Modern World*]. 1965. In *Vatican Council II: The Conciliar and Post-Conciliar Documents*. Ed. Austin Flannery, 903-1101. Wilmington, DE: Scholarly Resources.

Girard, René. 1979. *Violence and the Sacred*. Trans. Patrick Gregory. Baltimore: Johns Hopkins University Press.

_____. 1986. *The Scapegoat*. Trans. Yvonne Freccero. Baltimore: Johns Hopkins University Press.

_____. 1987a. *Job: The Victim of His People*. Stanford: Stanford University Press.

_____. 1987b. *Things Hidden Since the Foundation of the World*. Stanford: Stanford University Press.

Guzman, German. 1969. *Camilo Torres*. Trans. John D. Ring. New York: Sheed & Ward.

Hamerton-Kelly, Robert G. 1994. *The Gospel and the Sacred: Poetics of Violence in Mark*. Minneapolis: Fortress.

Heidegger, Martin. 1959. *An Introduction to Metaphysics*. New Haven: Yale University Press.

Heschel, Abraham J. 1966. "No Religion Is an Island." *Union Theological Seminary Quarterly* 21, no. 2: 1.

_____. 1969. "Reflections on Death." In *Genesi della morte improvisa e rianimazion* [*Genesis of Sudden Death and Reanimation*]. Ed. V. Lapiccirella. Papers presented in Florence, Palazzo Pitti, Oct. 14. Florence: Marchi & Bertolli.

John XXIII. 1963. *Pacem in Terris*. [*Peace on Earth*]. 11 April 1963. *Acta Apostolica Sedis*.

John Paul II. 1982. Homily at Bagington Airport, Coventry. *Origins* 2, no. 12: 55.

Lane, Belden C. 1988. *Landscapes of the Sacred: Geography and Narrative in American Spirituality*. New York: Paulist.

McKenna, Andrew J. 1992. *Violence and Difference*. Urbana: University of Illinois Press.

Merton, Thomas. 1971. *Thomas Merton on Peace*. New York: McCall.

Paul VI. 1967. *Populorum Progressio* [*On the Development of Peoples*]. 26 March, 1967. *Acta Apostolica Sedis*.

_____. 1975. *Evangelii Nuntiandi* [*Evangelization in the Modern World*]. 8 December 1975. *Acta Apostolica Sedis*.

Raper, Arthur F. 1969. *The Tragedy of Lynching*. New York: Arno.

Sharp, George. 1970. *Exploring Nonviolent Alternatives*. Boston: Porter Sargent.

Schwager, Raymond. 1987. *Must There Be Scapegoats?: Violence and Redemption in the Bible*. Trans. M. L. Assad. San Francisco: Harper & Row.

Tolnay, Stewart E., and E. M. Beck. 1995. *A Festival of Violence: An Analysis of Southern Lynchings, 1882-1930*. Urbana: University of Illinois Press.

United States Catholic Conference. 1983. *The Challenge of Peace: God's Promise and Our Response*. Washington, D.C.: USCC.

West, Charles. 1969. *Ethics, Violence, and Revolution*. New York: Council on Religion and International Affairs.

Williams, James G. 1991. *The Bible, Violence, and the Sacred: Liberation from the Myth of Sanctioned Violence*. San Francisco: Harper.

S A M U E L   P I S A R

Blood and Hope

Allow me to begin by saying, even though Auschwitz is not a place that lends itself to humor, that when my good friend, Rabbi Ehrenkranz, invited me to come back and speak here, the idea struck me as cruel and unusual punishment. I apologize also for the delayed arrival. Because of bad weather my flight from Paris was rerouted via Warsaw. It was a long and difficult journey, but not nearly as bad as the first one that brought me here fifty-five years ago in a cattle train. I remember that time as if it were yesterday; when the highly perishable cargo was unloaded, a good third of us were no longer alive. So I am not really complaining about today's trip.

Eminence, Excellencies, ladies and gentlemen, it is true that to return to this altar of the Holocaust, where I had once died so many deaths, suffered so many tortures and humiliations, where everything I had ever loved went up in smoke, is an experience that wrenches the soul. What makes it bearable, is that this time I am on a mission of hope, a mission in the service of humanity and God.

Your choice of Auschwitz for a world conference on "Religion and Violence, Religion and Peace," which has brought together so many eminent representatives of the three monotheistic faiths is pregnant with meaning. For here—I think I have the credentials to say it—we are in the presence of millions of innocent martyrs. I believe that if they could make themselves heard, they would let out a clamor towards you: "Never again!"

Your agenda focuses on many weighty issues, in particular the roots of violence in the world and the roots of peace in the Torah,

New Testament, and Qur'an. Yet this gigantic cemetery, which has neither graves nor tombstones, and where there should be no crosses, crescents, or stars, testifies to the inadequacy of our words, of our vocabularies, of our voices, and tends to make us numb. Even I hesitate to disturb the silence of those who perished here: Jews, Gypsies, Slavs and others, including my entire family.

If I am to contribute something meaningful to your deliberations, I must not address you in the muted tones of the modern man of affairs that I have become in my new incarnation; a product of great universities who lives and works in the glittering capitals of the world. I must also find within me the authentic voice of the young *untermensch,* the skeletal sub-human with a shaved head and sunken eyes, who started life in the ethnic cauldrons of Europe and was meant to give it up at the age of thirteen in the furnaces of Auschwitz, where Eichmann's grim reality eclipsed even Dante's imaginary vision of the Inferno.

From Hitler to Stalin, from Mao to Pol Pot, from the ethnic cleansing in Bosnia to the racist pogroms in Rwanda, and the religious massacres in Algeria, our century has been blood-stained by hideous crimes against humanity. Your pilgrimage to Auschwitz— the site of history's greatest genocide—for prayer and meditation on war and peace, on bigotry and tolerance, on the religious and moral values that can reclaim the world's alienated youth, is an enterprise of universal significance. Because, on these killing fields, we dare not forget that the past can also be prologue, that here we can discern the specter of doomsday, a warning to humankind, of what may still lie ahead.

To make the link between why we are here and what happened at this place half a century ago, permit me to tell you that I feel today in my bones: the fear, despair, and mounting anger at the heart of burning international issues that are debated coldly and impersonally by economists, diplomats, and politicians. All of these issues and horrors were present in this ugly microcosm that I knew so well at an early age.

Permit me to start with *hunger.* The gnawing starvation that sucks the will out of two-thirds of humankind and subjects entire continents to political and social convulsions is no abstraction for someone who had to grasp at whatever morsels he could find in order to hold onto a flicker of life. How do you convey to people who have led only a normal existence that constant, obsessive, hallucinating search for something to eat that overpowers all the senses and the mind?

Health care is one of the great issues of our time. For years we lived here in filth, promiscuity, and stench, packed into crowded barracks with other extenuated human beings, like cattle awaiting our turn in the slaughterhouse. Without hygiene, without drugs, without doctors, our only contact with "medicine" was the prospect of becoming guinea pigs for the infamous Dr. Joseph Mengele, the Angel of Death, and the other Nazi physicians who conducted atrocious experiments on their helpless victims.

Unemployment. Sending people to the death camps was a logical way to solve this problem. When we were not worked to exhaustion or death in the Reich's slave factories, we were made to perform before uniformed representatives of the "Master Race" for hours on end an elaborate "caps off" exercise. We were forced to march endlessly in place to test the durability of their army boots. Falling out of step meant a blow that cracked open one's skull.

Human rights? I witnessed innocents by the thousands condemned to execution on the spot. I saw families dismembered, girls raped, women, children and old people sent to the ovens, and able-bodied men placed in bondage—their death merely deferred. *Habeas corpus,* trial by jury and all the other constitutional guarantees that we take so much for granted, are like sacred talismans for me today. Every act of arbitrary justice conjures up in my mind the dark road back to the abyss.

The Third World. I hold the conviction that we must come to see the people of the underprivileged countries as brothers and sisters to be succored in the name of common humanity, rather than faceless masses best left to flounder in their own misery. That conviction comes very naturally to someone who was once among the disinherited and the despised.

Terrorism. The methods of its current practitioners scarcely differ from the ground rules that prevailed here, when hostages were taken and shot routinely for no other reason than to sow panic and fear. The slightest deviance, the smallest gesture of disobedience was perceived by our hangmen as a threat to their perverse law and order, and punished by instant death.

Democracy. My family and I came to know exile, martial law, daily curfews, and the dreaded midnight knock on the door. The only freedom of assembly, association, and speech we enjoyed was the macabre roll calls at dawn and dusk and the right to shout, "Present!" Does democracy really have the will to survive or merely to throw off a few more brilliant sparks, like a dead star flaring up briefly at the end of its journey? The shocks that buffet our societies and threaten to dislocate our economies and our governments could once again tempt silent majorities to surrender political power to bloodthirsty dictators and tyrants.

The arms race. Despite the end of the Cold War, the feverish construction of ever more sophisticated nuclear, chemical, and biological weapons goes on and on as if to ensure that there will always be adequate means for a final solution. The Nazis conducted intensive research to find the most deadly and least costly poisons. Today, other rogue regimes have resumed their work. The innocent victims who were herded into Auschwitz's gas chambers—I saw it with my own eyes—had but three minutes to live once the doors were closed. Yet somehow they had sufficient time and strength to dig their fingernails into the walls and scratch the words, "Never forget." Have we already forgotten?

Peace. I know that some people consider peace as an undesirable condition. War can reshuffle the cards, sweep away the whole mess of unbearable, seemingly insoluble problems. When it is over, we can make a fresh start, inject a new vitality into the economic system; shattered towns and industries can be rebuilt and modernized; and ambitious entrepreneurs with energy, daring, and greed can start new careers and generate new wealth.

Religion. How many millions have been murdered in the name of religion! The heavens remained strangely silent here while the crematoria were belching fire and smoke. Where was God, where was the Pope? Did anyone out there know what was happening to us here? Did they care? I ask for your indulgence, but I must confess that there were moments when, in my childish innocence and despair, I would raise a clenched, blasphemous fist toward the Almighty. We Jews had been condemned to oblivion for no other reason than our blood was tainted. I remember as a young boy lying at night on my aching back in the freezing barracks and thinking to myself that if the Lord Jesus Christ had lived in my time, he, his mother Mary, his siblings, and all the Twelve Apostles would have been with me here at Auschwitz, because their blood was as tainted as mine.

The Nazis saw in religion, as in learning and culture, typical Jewish traits. Paraphrasing Nietzsche, they decreed that if the Judeo-Christian God was dead, if Judaic-Christian law and morality were abrogated, then the mythical Teutonic supermen, the Wagnerian knights of the *Niebelungen*, would become the new deities.

As they proceeded to fulfill this pagan prophecy, they maimed their own nation as well as others. There were one-and-a-half million children among the six million Jews who died, including the 500 children of my own school, of which I am literally the sole survivor. These were the children who never learned, the teachers who never taught, the scientists who never discovered, the poets who never wrote. These were the children who would have so greatly enriched our world if they had lived. By placing the sins of the world on Jewish shoulders, certain Christian thinkers and inquisitors had turned their backs on Christ himself, opening the way to persecution, mayhem, and in the end, the Holocaust.

Karol Wojtyla came from a country on whose living body was inflicted the massive wound of Auschwitz. He was born and brought up in the vicinity of this wound, and his ascent to the throne of St. Peter was not unrelated to his origins. He must have felt the weight of all this whenever he recalled the classroom he had shared with Jewish children a few miles from here. After the Pope led an immense crowd to Auschwitz in 1979, calling it the "Golgotha of the Modern World," he later announced to the world in 1980: "The *Shoah* is an experience which I carry within me." Subsequently he crossed the Tiber River in 1986 to pray at a Roman synagogue. Although I am not of his parish, I believe that what he had witnessed in his youth from the other side of this barbed-wire fence will cause him to continue to speak out against the poisonous roots of religious and anti-Semitic violence that fuels such genocidal nightmares.

Dear friends, we have gathered here out of respect for each other's faith. Jointly, Christians, Muslims, and Jews, we must beware of what we preach to our respective flocks because we are what we preach, and because fundamentalism, fanaticism, dogmatism, and all ideologies that despise the human being could push our societies toward a new delirium of violence. In the name of peace, which is your principal theme here, let us turn for inspiration to the comforting, rather than the gruesome lessons of the past. On this continent, after the first millennium, a momentary Jewish, Islamic, and Christian symbiosis had propelled Spain and the rest of the Iberian Peninsula to its so-called "Golden Age." Sharing the heritage of Abraham, all three communities were teeming with scholars, philosophers, poets, musicians, and statesmen. It did not last long. That noble, however short-lived experience, allows us to dream of harmony in the future.

There is also contemporary evidence that religious, racial, or national divergence does not necessarily breed hereditary enemies forever. Astounding recent events have shown how seemingly hardened, historic hostility between peoples can give way to constructive coexistence. If Germans and French, Japanese and Chinese, Americans and Russians, or blacks and whites in formerly apartheid Africa can choose peace, then why not Irish Catholics and English Protestants? Indeed, why not Palestinians and Jews?

At the invitation of King Hussein II of Morocco, forty dignitaries from Islam, Judaism, and Christianity met in February of this year. They declared that all forms of intolerance, discrimination, and violence are contrary to the message of fraternity and peace emanating from the Holy Scriptures of the three monotheistic religions.

Israel is currently celebrating its fiftieth anniversary as an independent nation reborn from the ashes, reborn in its promised land. From the slavery in Egypt, the Babylonian captivity, the Roman conquest, the Spanish Inquisition, the Czarist pogroms, and of course, the Nazi Holocaust, I ask you who could have imagined such a miracle after all the tragedies that have been visited upon the Jewish people since time immemorial? Who can deny that the miracle of Israeli-Palestinian peace is now really in gestation?

We, the survivors who have experienced in our flesh and our souls the greatest catastrophe that ever befell human civilization, are now disappearing one by one. Soon history will begin to speak, at best, with the impersonal voices of researchers, academics, and novelists; at worst, with the malevolent voices of revisionists and falsifiers. But as long as we are here, we must bear witness and hand down our legacy to all humanity, Jews and Gentiles alike. We who have lived know that the human animal is capable of the worst and the best, madness and genius. We know that when humans lose their moral compass, their faith in God, the unthinkable becomes possible.

Even as we meet here in Auschwitz, we can hear xenophobic, racist, neo-fascist vituperation in various parts of this fratricidal continent and the world beyond. And as we listen to it, we are reminded of Bertolt Brecht's warning: "Beware, the womb that carried the dreadful beast is still fertile."

Mercifully, the attitude of the Roman Catholic Church toward Judaism began to change under Pope John XXIII. Pope John Paul II went further and made improved Christian-Jewish relations a central concern of his pontificate. Under his impetus, the Vatican took a serious first step to recant its institutionalized antagonism towards God's chosen people and to condemn its silence and passivity during the murderous Nazi era as a sin. The Catholic bishops of Germany, France, Poland, and other European countries have also made impressive, even greater *mea culpas*. These are encouraging beginnings, but the process of teaching and of healing must be accelerated and strengthened by the concerted action of all religions if the age-old violence is to be stopped once and for all.

If I have allowed myself to step out of the normal and contented life I lead today and anaesthetize myself sufficiently to come back to Auschwitz; if I have allowed my memories to speak, to invoke the blood of the past and the hope for the future that has nourished my confidence in humanity's capacity for endurance and redemption, it is because our children and grandchildren need to know the truth. They need to arm themselves spiritually against the tragedies, the hypocrisies and the false gods of history. They need to ensure that what happened here at the heart of

Christian, civilized, cultured Europe in the middle of the twentieth century will never happen again.

May myriad sermons and deeds be inspired by this cursed and sacred place and by the shared religious values that you will confirm here in the coming days. May all of this help to lead humanity to greater compassion, tolerance, and peace.

ELISABETH MAXWELL

Anger and Courage:
A Reply to Samuel Pisar

I fear that silence is the only possible response to what we have just heard. Perhaps the first words I can utter are, "*Mea Culpa, Mit brennender Sorge, Jal, Smutek, Rhaach-mim, Raarch-moonis.*" We beg God's pardon, and we call upon the Jewish people to hear our words of repentance.

It was Elie Wiesel who entitled his collected writings *Against Silence* and inspired me to speak out openly about the Holocaust. That is why today I have agreed to reply to the opening address of my long-loved and revered friend, Samuel Pisar.

A few days ago, on the other side of the Atlantic, my mentor and friend, the Christian theologian Roy Eckhardt, died. "He was one of the very best, most sensitive, most moving interpreters of Jewish life and all that is related to it, including the tragedies which people endured," said Wiesel. Of the theologians I have met and known, he was the most outstanding and the most profound and original thinker, a man of total integrity. He was in my eyes a model of moral and intellectual courage, both in his rejection of those aspects of Christian theology which he could no longer accept, and in his defense of the Jews at a time when neither of these stances was acceptable.

It was also Roy who transformed my life on our first encounter some fifteen years ago, when study of the Holocaust had left me profoundly anxious about the tenets of my own Protestant faith. He was largely responsible for my conversion (the right word in this context), not to Judaism, but to a reformed and enlightened Christianity from which all forms of anti-

Semitism and supersessionism have been removed and listening to "the other" has become almost axiomatic. Roy listened to me with patience, answered my questions, and calmed my anxieties with great simplicity and wisdom. "The real issue," he said, "is what is the right thing to do? The challenge is not whether to be labeled a Christian or a non-Christian; it is how to be human, how to be responsible. Just do what is right and good in the sight of the Lord. To accomplish the task you have set for yourself, you need anger and you need courage." From that moment, all became clear to me, and I never looked back.

I hope, Your Eminences, that you will show indulgence towards one who is not of your flock, but a descendant of a proud and formerly persecuted minority, the French Huguenots. Perhaps you will be moved to learn that my mother was a Roman Catholic who was excommunicated when she married into a strict Huguenot family and did not promise that her children would be Catholic but was pardoned twenty years later by Pope Pius XI, and her excommunication was lifted.

To complete my ecumenism, I married a Jew whose own family, almost to the last member, was murdered in this very death camp; not only his parents, grandparents, and five siblings, but 500 of his relations. They arrived here on one of the last transports from Hungary in 1944, fifty years ago practically to the day. They were gassed on arrival and their bodies burned in the woods over there. By that time immensely courageous inmates had managed to blow up one of the crematoria and such was the massive intake of victims, that they could no longer cope with burning the bodies in the remaining crematoria.

I cannot believe that any one of us here today has not made his or her own *mea culpa* and act of contrition; otherwise it would not be possible to tread the earth of Auschwitz. That is not to imply that we are personally guilty, but Christians, Muslims, and Jews must bear the responsibility of our own creeds and examine with an honest heart what went wrong in our teaching, in our deafness, when the voices of the martyrs cried out for help.

I am certain, too, that all those who gather here today do so in a spirit of goodwill and have made this great effort to come so far in order to go forward together. This is truly no place for politics or polemics, for arrogance or supersessionism. It is the time and place to search our consciences, to repent and seek God's guidance and blessing on our deliberations; and above all, to recall the words of Deuteronomy, "To do what is right and good in the sight of the Lord." For this is a place where we cannot hide behind lies.

In answer to Sam Pisar's question as a child inmate in this camp, "Did anyone out there know what was happening to us here? Did they care?" We have to confess, "Yes, we knew." As the German army advanced into the Soviet Union, the Allied governments knew what the *Einsatzgruppen* were doing to the two-and-a-half million Russian and Ukrainian Jews. The British Secret Service had broken the German military code; they were able to read reports and informed Churchill directly of the daily murders, quoting exact statistics of men, women, and children shot in makeshift pits. The whole world was aware, as has been abundantly demonstrated. But in the words of the American Christian, Hubert Locke, "All that was heard was the deafening silence of the Church." We knew and did nothing. The Allies could not be moved even to bomb the railway lines which led to Auschwitz, although Allied bombers flew every night only a few minutes away from here, bombing arms factories in Eastern Germany and Czechoslovakia.

First, in the words of the 1998 Vatican statement, *We Remember: A Reflection on the Shoah*, it is honest and proper to examine "the ways in which the image of the Creator in man has been offended and disfigured," and to recognize that "the balance of our relations with the Jews over 2,000 years has been quite negative." Indeed, we have to accept that anti-Jewish prejudices were imbedded in most Christian minds and hearts through the teaching and false interpretations of the gospels spread by some of the early fathers of our faith. Because of this widespread anti-Semitism, Christians did not give every possible assistance to those being persecuted, in this case, the Jews. As the statement concludes: "We wish to turn awareness of past sins into a firm resolve to build a new future in which there will be no more anti-Judaism among Christians or anti-Christian sentiment among Jews, but rather a shared mutual respect as befits those who adore the one Creator and Lord and have a common Father in faith, Abraham."

This brings me to address the representatives of Islam, the third monotheistic faith, third in chronology, that is. I must confess to being extremely ignorant about your religion, because, once again, my past education, both religious and secular, conveniently chose to overlook Islam as a faith, although in history I was taught about the great Ottoman Empire. I will, therefore, listen to your discussions here with great interest, wishing to be enlightened and refusing to accept all the myths and stereotyped teachings which have done the world so much harm. We have much to learn from you and perhaps we can share with you our bitter experience of the evil that can result from false teachings and mass hysteria. Perhaps we can also hear how you perceive us, where you think we are going wrong at the present time, and how you can help us to change the demonic perception of the world of Islam that Christians and Jews alike now have, or indeed, we may help you to change the equally demonic perception of the Jewish world which has made its way into the Arab world.

I am not a theologian or historian, nor a philosopher, economist, or sociologist. I am an educator and, above all, a disseminator. I have recently been elected Chair of Remembering for the Future 2000, an international conference of scholars who take the *Shoah* as the center of their reflections. We will meet in the year 2000 to agree on the kind of memory and lessons which should be handed down to the generations of the coming century. For post-Holocaust thinking must take fully into account the fact that the second half of the twentieth century has inaugurated a new era in human self-awareness and human possibility, an era capable of producing unprecedented destruction or unparalleled hope. We now know that we have the power to destroy humanity and are finally aware of the challenge of human survival.

Major twentieth-century scientific advances, particularly the quantum, computer, and biomolecular revolutions, have together given scientists unprecedented power. But it is incumbent on us all to ensure that such technological wonders are put to proper use and that an ethical code of human behavior still rules our lives.

We must all heed the lessons of the twentieth century and ensure that such developments are used, not in the cause of destruction, but in a positive spirit towards the conservation of our world, the advancement of the social order, and a more equal society with love of one's neighbor at its heart.

In Sam Pisar's prophetic words, "We dare not forget that the past can also be prologue, that here we can discern the specter of doomsday, a warning to mankind." I would also add a warning to us here of what might still lie ahead if we cannot achieve an earnest and fraternal statement of our common belief in the one God. Whether we reach God through the prophets, holy ones, saints, or through the mediation of Jesus Christ, we must work together with a common determination to arm the coming generations of the world, not with guns and grenades but with spiritual, religious, and moral knowledge against the false gods of the modern age and the wisdom to allow our neighbors to be different.

Works Cited

Commission for Religious Relations with the Jews. 16 March, 1998. *We Remember: A Reflection on the Shoah*. Vatican City: Libreria Editrice Vaticana.

Wiesel, Elie. 1985. *Against Silence*. Irving Abrahamson, ed. New York: Holocaust Library.

MARTIN E. MARTY

Fundamentalism as a
Precursor to Violence

My assigned topic, "Fundamentalism as a Precursor to Violence," assumes that fundamentalism is or can be such a precursor. I accept the assignment and the topic and share the assumption. This means that the keynote has a thesis: to understand more dimensions of violence in the world today, it is valuable to understand what the word "fundamentalism" designates; under what circumstances its various manifestations do—or at least can—relate, especially as a "precursor" to violence; and to begin to grasp some of the reasons why it does so, as a step toward addressing the problems such a relation brings.

The words "fundamentalism" and "precursor" are sufficiently complex to exhaust us. This is not the conference address in which we must examine all the dimensions of "violence." Suffice it to say here that in its most extreme form fundamentalism issues in terrorism, military action, or murder. Short of that, violence can create civil disorder and uncivil conduct in nonlethal forms that can take a toll on personal and communal health. Words kill. Dismissal of "the stranger" from the circles of civil conversation is distracting and destructive, as is demeaning or devastating "the other" in a community—be it familial, religious, social, or political. So fundamentalism, in all its forms that are productive of any types of violence, confronts us as a phenomenon demanding examination by all who seek a world in which "religion and peace" as a theme and a reality has its place.

Fundamentalism: I wish we could hurry past the term in order to get at the effects of the phenomenon that the conference planners wish us to explore in depth. Unfortunately, such hurrying is a luxury disallowed among people in fields of statecraft, communication, intergroup relations, religious leadership, and ordinary everyday citizenship. After leading conferences and editing books on the subject for a period of years, I would cite the following as elements to keep in mind:

- "Fundamentalism" is a term born in North American Protestant controversy in the twentieth century. Not all members or observers of movements elsewhere would have chosen that term or find it congenial or in all respects accurate when applied in other contexts.

- The word has traveled, however, and is used generically, just as other words that have traveled from the West to the world (or vice versa) have migrated, acquiring new characteristics and expressions of cognate, but not identical, features elsewhere. One thinks of terms such as "liberal," "conservative," "orthodox," "nationalist," "capitalist," "republican," "democratic," "socialist," and the like.

- When using the word "fundamentalism"—after one has treated the difficulties of definition and then begun to define it—it is important to be sensitive to those who participate in or report on those cognate movements elsewhere. One may think of "fundamentalism" and then speak of "fundamentalist-like" movements or of movements that "bear family resemblances to fundamentalism." Where time and circumstances permit, one might even track words of other origin—for example, Hebrew or Arabic—to speak of movements that have risen in cultures far removed from Anglophonic Protestantism.

- Whenever one uses the generic term "fundamentalism," it is important to remember that the use of terms for comparative purposes is necessary, but they have to be handled with care. Unless one classifies or typifies, certain features of movements do not stand out in bold relief. But when one deals with categories and types, it is also possible to overlook particularities, distinctive, and even contradictory elements in each movement. The more one studies fundamentalisms, the more apparent it becomes that substantively they may have little in common with each other. Their inventors, adherents, and propagators will have declared their fundamentalist-like commitments in order to differentiate themselves from all others. These others may include those within their own religious communities who deviate even the slightest from what a fundamentalism is supposed to be "about" or who as moderates cross boundaries between the community and others. Thus, Protestant fundamentalism has tended to be doctrinal above all, while Catholic fundamentalism has concentrated on magisterial churchly teaching, as in nineteenth-century papal documents. Jewish fundamentalist movements concentrate on story (for example, its constituents like to tell stories of how God promised a specific land to Abraham and Moses and assured conquest through Joshua). And in Islam, the accent is on law and the literal application of laws in *shari'ah*, the body of law that appears as a kind of commentary on the Qur'an.

With those precautions in mind, we turn to a rationale for the use of such a term as fundamentalism in the first place, and then we point, as phenomenologists more than lexicographers might, to some features. For brevity's sake, we again highlight:

- Fundamentalism is not the same as orthodoxy, traditionalism, classicism, or conservatism, designations for phenomena that had existed for centuries before the twentieth. ("Fundamentalism" does not appear in lexicons of earlier centuries, as the other forms do.) One may begin naively and ask: Given such terms, why was a new set of them necessary, or why did partisans, their enemies, and observers find it valuable to coin new words? Quite likely, the coiners of the terms, those who opposed them, and those who reported on them were dealing with a new phenomenon, one that needed new designations. As a matter of record, while in more recent decades fundamentalism is often seen to be used pejoratively, it was originally chosen for the banners around which people were to rally. It was a badge of honor. Thus in the 1920s, Presbyterians and Baptists in the United States, torn by division over doctrine, heard that while many wanted to be called to be conservative or traditional, conservatives and traditionalists did not "do battle for the Lord." Fundamentalists would exist precisely to do that.

- Religious fundamentalisms, subsequently, have come to be seen as modern movements, movements reactive (though not always reactionary) to the challenges presented by a world described and seen as modern and characterized by second-order words such as "modernization," "modernity," and "modernism." Thus they are not what we might call fossilized movements, ossified in strata where the marks of earlier forms of existence thrived. They are not "the old time religion," though they borrow marks of it. Modern religious fundamentalisms, as some of us in the United States have differentiated them from forms that bore resemblance to them in all religions through many ages, are movements that rose after academicians, mass communicators, and elites in the Western and post-Enlightenment world thought there would be no more of such. Heirs of the Enlightenment often acted reflexively, as if religion itself would diminish and its forces would wane or any surviving religious movements would be enlightened, concessive, wan, tolerant, and reconciling. Instead, religion seemed to survive with a vengeance and to spawn movements that prospered precisely to the degree that they were uncompromising, their adherents absolutist and zealous.

- Modernity and modernization, of course, mean many things. But the observer of fundamentalism sees them as the occasion for pluralism in polities where one religious regime had been dominant, if not monopolistic. As a corollary, the presence of "the other" and of so many others—especially from outside, as in the case of "imperial" forces—tended to tempt citizens into relativism about truth, story, and behavior. And modernism tended to refer to religious, sometimes theological, adaptations by moderates and compromisers from within one's larger community of faith. Fundamentalisms reacted against pluralism, relativism, moderation, and attendant corruptions of the ideal; fundamentalisms reacted and turned militant in various ways.

- Where do the "fundamentals" of fundamentalism come in? They are elements of doctrine, story, law, or whatever else that are retrieved—"selectively retrieved," some of us want to say—for use as defense against enemies of the movement or for aggression where the movement would expand. Traditionalists, conservatives, and the orthodox want to keep vital the whole of a tradition as they receive and perceive it. Fundamentalists would say that they do, and in good faith, when pressed, they can come forth with professions of assent to the whole of the tradition. But for tactical and psychological reasons, they tend to be more efficient and to be selective. They choose what helps them fight their cause. Traditionalists, conservatives, and the orthodox are busy with the whole; they tend to mind their own business and let others pass them by. They do not "do battle for the Lord." (To take an illustration from the complex I know best, American Protestantism, most Christians would list the Trinity and the sacraments as the fundamentals, yet they rarely have come up in Protestant fundamentalist definition. In part this is the case because fundamentalists disagree with each other about the sacraments and would find witness to the Trinity too complex, vague, and beside the point for their battles. It is easy to find parallel illustrations in Judaism and Islam.)

- Finally, given the need for reaction against threats to one's personal and social identity; having ordered a movement that creates boundaries and distance from "the other"; having chosen fundamentalistic approaches as defenses against modernity, what is next? Most movements see themselves as chosen, as elect instruments to carry out divine purposes as they have been instructed to do in sacred writings, or as recapturing ideal moments in the past. They use this chosenness or election against "the other." They know where history is going. This is one reason why the "peoples of the book," the prophetic and often *telos*-centered people in Abrahamic and Jerusalemaic movements, find it easier to define their fundamentals and be fundamentalists than those in religions which make less of the book (for example, Buddhisms) or have diffuse scriptures and, in Western terms, pantheons with which to deal (for example, Hinduisms). It is only the forms, those we have just called prophetic, that are the concern of this conference. However, their destiny in the globe today has to be understood in the face of fundamentalisms that are rising and being named in Hinduism, Sikhism, and the like.

So much for fundamentalism and violence. What about fundamentalism as a precursor of violence? We have to spend at least a moment on the concept of the precursive. At root, such terms derive from the Old French *cours* and the Latin *cursus*, from *currere*, to run. So the idea here is to see in what ways fundamentalism "runs before" or "runs ahead of" violence. For some reason "postcursive" has not entered the English vocabulary. If it had, it might mean, in our case, that violence breaks out on, say, nonreligious terms, and fundamentalists attach themselves to the causes that engendered it, providing justifications for such violence. Instances of this are available in numerous twentieth-century situations, where war breaks out for any number of reasons—economic, ethnic, territorial, and the like—and gets legitimated and even propelled by fundamentalists on one side or both. Thus during Russian military action in Chechnya, the Chechnyans began to attach green (for Islam) ribbons to armament. I am not able to say that these Chechnyans were fundamentalist, but they were selectively retrieving dormant and latent symbols from their tradition and making it visible. Protestant fundamentalists in the United States have on occasion been the militant superpatriots, suspicious of those seen as less so, for example against the "Evil Empire" in the years of the Cold War. The Cold War was not begun or fostered as a prime item on Protestant fundamentalist agendas, but many fundamentalists became prime sustainers of the conflict.

Just as the postcursive is not the keynote topic, neither is the concursive. If in the former, fundamentalisms would run behind expressions of violence, so in the concurrent case, they would run with or flow alongside outbreaks of violence that would have an independent life apart from modern religious fundamentalism. In some cases, fundamentalists would exploit such moments to advance their own cause, to rally their own troops, to build their own defenses and armaments. But in many nationalist circumstances, they might also so identify the nationalist purposes with God's and their agenda, with purification of God's elect nation, that they become allies with secular or other religious forces.

For example, surely the modern state of Israel is not the product of precursive American Protestant fundamentalists. It was born of the activity of Zionism and a variety of pioneering movements, just as it was an expression of nationalism by peoples left out of the inventions of modern European nationalisms around 1870. (Germany, Italy, and the like took shape then.) Zionism had its own course and was following it. But it happened that American Protestant fundamentalism, as it was taking shape during and after World War I, was in most cases premillennial, apocalyptic, and messianic. Its leadership dipped into ancient prophetic writings and applied them literally to the Israel that they hoped would come into being and then, after World War II, to the Israel that was established. Such Protestant fundamentalists often became the most fervent and unyielding supporters of Israel, though not for the reasons that Israeli Zionists or nationalists were. They were concursive, "flowing alongside of each other," and never merging currents in twentieth-century international politics.

It is not the question of postcursive or concursive activity that provides our central focus. We are to ask in what ways modern religious fundamentalism is or can be a precursor of violence. Posed this way, the issue pushes us back to precursive questions, particularly, What is it about religion, and especially fundamentalism, that it can serve both to heal and to kill?

Raising that question leads to the need for expressing an urgent qualification and reserve. One does this for the sake of precise definition, clarity, precision, fairness to all involved, and strategy. Not all fundamentalisms and fundamentalists necessarily are precursors of violence, at least not in the form of military or terrorist belligerencies. There are fundamentalists who "mind their own business" and appear to be little more than especially rigorous and rigid conservatives. Thus, in the United States, a classic fundamentalist college is Bob Jones University. Its leaders would be insulted if they were seen to be in any way concessive, compromising, or anything else less than fundamentalistically firm. Yet, while Bob Jones has had to be legally and psychologically militant in defense of its segregationist policies against the federal administration of law—a militancy that many, especially African-Americans, can credibly point out is its own form of verbal and psychological violence—its leadership steadfastly tries to avoid political comment or engagement. It does not take much social scientific research or many finely tuned antennae for those who know the Bob Jones people to surmise that as citizens most of them are politically and economically ultraconservative. But as a people, in corporate ways, they do not turn militant or violent. Great numbers of fundamentalists are simply "ordinary citizens," going about their business in the laboratory, the computer center, the supermarket, or the polling place without manifesting features that are even potential expressions of violence.

These "ordinary citizens" dare not be forgotten by anyone who wants to understand everything about fundamentalism, but they are not our current subjects. Our assignment calls for a focus on those fundamentalisms that are born to be, or turn out to be, violent in ways precursive to their involvement in warfare or terrorism.

In order to understand the world of fundamentalists, the leadership of the Fundamentalist Project in the United States in the late 1980s and early 1990s hypothesized the characteristic behaviors, affiliations, and beliefs of an individual fundamentalist. We asked what was at stake. One way to do this was to picture his or her set of "worlds" as concentric spheres of meaning, awareness, and activity.

Thus, closest to the individual is his worldview, that personalized, always changing, but irreplaceable center of the ego. Here is where the religious self is concentrated. One is "enlightened" as a Buddhist, "born again" as an evangelical, "converted" in any faith, and cannot easily become other-enlightened, born again again, deconverted, or reconverted. If one does become so, it means a drastic alteration in the worldview, the self. Much of the impulse for fundamentalist outlook and action is located in this center of the ego.

From there one moves out, as we must do hurriedly here, to concentric spheres. Observers of the world scene would likely agree that second would be the issue of personal identity. Who am I?—which means also, To whom do I belong? Who belongs to me? Who are my people? On whom can I count and whom do I trust? Of whom must I be suspicious? This set of questions relates closely to what many call "tribalism," which survives or takes new intense shapes in late modernity.

The next sphere might well have to do with gender, sexuality, and such social forms as the family. Most fundamentalists are at odds with moderns who would complicate traditional expressions of gender, engage in sexual revolution, or relativize, if not denigrate, the family. In all the cultures we have studied, these intimate zones of life provide the platform and program for what have come to be called "social issues." Defending these is not ordinarily the first cause that issues in military forms of violence. But on verbal and other communicative levels—including politics— these "social issues," when fundamentalistically defended, can go beyond the argument on which politics must thrive and give rise to forms of attack disruptive of civil order.

The next spheres, a bit further from egocentrality, would have to do with the worlds of health and illness, the laboratory and the clinic, the sphere where biological issues meet the spiritual. Especially in wealthy industrial societies where the instruments of medical technology make possible in vitro fertilization or physician-assisted suicide, fundamentalists will fight over the issues of the body. Similarly, education represents a zone for conflict. If one believes something passionately and belongs to a people that also does, there is a need to propagate the outlook, beginning at home with one's own next generation. In all the fundamentalist cultures, there are either creations of self-protective schools or battlers for fundamentalist witness in public schools.

Mass media represent another sphere. All the other revolutions of modernity, pluralism, and relativism are borne to the individual by such media of communication. They are almost always subversive. Unless one engages in acts of distancing as strenuous as those of the Amish in America or the hyperorthodox Jews in Williamsburg or Jerusalem, it is virtually impossible to keep radio, television, film, books, magazines, and the like away from the children especially or the sensitive in a fundamentalist community. For that reason, what is broadcast or published becomes controversial. Fundamentalists in several cultures situate themselves strategically on library boards, school boards, and the like. Or they compete and fashion media signals and empires that will distract from those that are subversive of fundamentalist faith, ethos, and community.

Only at this stage does it come to the spheres of economics, politics, constitutionalism, war, and terrorism. And they are often social forms of pooled individual interests or public expressions of private faith and practice. Economics turns out to be the least decisive and definitive, except in some Shi'ite Islamic fundamentalist movements where prescriptions against the taking of interest are features. Most fundamentalists are opposed to regimes that they would control, or picture that they once did, or that they see as destructive and even demonic, in which cases they may sound violently antigovernmental and may take military action against those in power. But others have settled for some form of discontented life within pluralism, being more interested in having a large say in how a polity is run. They want influence in it and protection from what they see to be malign elements.

Here is where politics and constitutionalism can come in. Fundamentalists may well try to effect their ways within these, confining violent impulses to the verbal and the organizational—all the while, it is to be said, as they face counterfundamentalists who are violent but not in armed ways. Finally, when fundamentalists express themselves in military or terrorist ways, the worlds of media, statecraft, and civilian citizenship pay attention. Here is the zone or sphere in which fundamentalists "make news" and disturb the peace at the century's end. What has concerned many of us who study the movements, to say nothing of those in them, is that attention often gets paid to the violent expression but not to the impulses closest to heart, soul, and mind that stand behind them.

Let me give one illustration. During the prolonged Iran-Iraq war, there were stories in the world press of Shi'ite Muslim fundamentalist mothers who authorized, or even sent, their ten-year-old sons to lock arms with others and walk over landmined fields, where they would almost certainly be blown up. All this was part of military action, since troops could now advance against the enemy unthreatened by mines. The rest of the world saw this as a simple expression of *jihad*, the holy cause or war. The mothers were portrayed then as heartless fanatics who cared for the cause but not their sons, who seemed to be mere objects in the lethal chess game of mindless war.

Whoever knew or studied such mothers at close hand would have to say that such an interpretation, while credible, was out of context. These were women in a mourning culture who, as long as they lived, would grieve the sons who, in their belief, were now in paradise. They cared as much as mothers anywhere. They did not "become Muslim" in order to blow up their sons or be violent in any way. They grew up in Islam and no doubt knew no alternatives and enjoyed the blessings of what they perceived as its gifts: peace, beneficence, benignity, meaning, ritual, and hope. The sacrifice of the son, while heart-wrenching, was not seen as contradictory to the saving, salutary, and health-providing dimensions of Islam. Whoever does not understand such particulars is not likely to comprehend how, in the fundamentalist world, the same religion can be both healer and killer. Consequently, there is not likely to be much positive address to the situation on the part of those who would have the healing, reconciling, and peacemaking side of a faith, of all faiths, of faith itself, prevail for the benefit of all peoples.

In parts of the world where most religion is ecumenical, tolerant, and concessive, at least when untested, it may be hard to conceive of religion as both killer and healer. There citizens tend to see religion as part of the same median zones of life, where public and private intersect. There one finds one among many centers of meaning and belonging, alongside others who do the same with other sets of such centers. In the process, in liberal cultures, religious reasoning has to share place with other forms, usually called something like "secular rationality." In such cultures, people have learned to be tolerant of others to the point of their seeing religious commitment as mere preference and arbitrary choice, to the point of its breeding indifference. Individualism reigns, as it does not in fundamentalist collectives. Religion in the United States gets domesticated and alphabetized safely in the "Churches and Synagogues" section of the Yellow Pages of the phone book, where it is often seen as safe to the point of blandness and boring—certainly not capable of issuing in violence (or, one might say, capable of promoting healing and peace!).

One must almost go back to basics to understand the fundamentalist religious impulse. While the fundamentalists we have interviewed would not use social scientific terms, one can listen to them and translate to such without doing violence to them. Thus they do not speak of the "corrosive threats of modernity to their personal and social identity." They do not talk about defending that which is of their "ultimate concern." They do not see themselves engaging in "selective retrieval" in order to find fundamentals that can be weapons against assaults to their faith, worldview, and community. They say, "I found it!" or "I am born again!" or "Allah is great!" or "Hear, O Israel!" or "I became enlightened!" Abstracting from these expressions, we see some common elements precursive to fundamentalism's potential as precursor to violence.

First, religion in intense forms is borne of some sense of awe. "Take the shoes off your feet, for the ground on which you are standing is holy ground!" (Exodus 3). This is the *mysterium tremendum et fascinans* of which the students of religion spoke and speak. One cannot be talked out of the experience. It produces for the confronted one a "world more real than the real world." And the voice of the unconsumed burning bush, or what is heard after the whirlwind or earthquake or crucifixion ("Surely this man was the Son of God!") cannot be denied. Not to respond is an impossibility.

That experience of awe, whether from the heart's promptings or stimulated by a charismatic leader or a confrontation with a scripture, leads to some sort of break with other reality. The non-religious or "secular" and the religious in other expressions become "the other" and are then seen as wrong, ignorant, unenlightened, willfully distanced, untruthful, inimical, and even demonic. But before one takes action against such, there must be a positive response. "Here am I, send me!" "I will submit," which is what Islam means and is about. "Go into all the world and preach the gospel." "Let my people go!"

With such negative and positive charges, there must be empowerment. The divine voice, from without or within, both authorizes a mission and guarantees that the speaker, the authorizer, will not abandon the respondent. Empowerment may come to an individual who becomes a mystic or contemplative. But more frequently it impels the one who has experienced awe and revelation to seek community. Such community extends the power, confirms the vision, provides company, and helps assure that the receipt of the empowerment was not idiosyncratic. So the community acquires the mission. And on the mission, adherents find that they confront the other as enemy: Pharaoh, Canaan, "the uncircumcised," the heathen and pagan, the Great Satan, the secular humanist, the infidel, the religious modernist, the alien mass communicator, and Big Government can all play such roles.

Those who act intensely, fanatically, exclusively of the other, and against the other are not "making this all up." Fundamentalisms in their selective retrieval have little difficulty finding warrior deities in the founding myths of the various faiths who urge them on. Because myths concentrate human experience and push the edges of mystery, they tend to have a double character. Those who seek peace and reconciliation have to acknowledge that locked into most such myths is an underside, a negation of the other. We may wish this feature away, but it will not go away. It is crucial to find ways to deal with the whole of the myth or story in such ways that it is not glossed over or overlooked or blithely explained away. It will return, to haunt; it will be brought up by the astute enemy.

Thus fundamentalist (and other) Christians have had no trouble finding legitimation in New Testament texts for violence alongside the great calls for peace and reconciliation. The books of Joshua and Judges include texts that also call for more than genocide. The Qur'an, which like the New Testament and Torah includes passages of great beauty and benignity, along with other basic Islamic texts, also licenses and impels militant action. Omnicide, *jihad*, crusade, inquisition: these are locked into stories revelatory of the deity.

The fundamentalist, not uniquely but in distinctive ways, is more prone than others to be a precursor to the violent, and we can now see why. The moderate, the liberal, and the modernist have been called or have chosen to be situated in ways more open to pluralism and more ready to take risks with relativism or the positive mien and voice of "the other." They negotiate with modernity on more open terms than does the fundamentalist who, in literalist fashion, adheres to and expresses sides of the myth and tradition that turn out to be lethal. They are more ready to question that which induces awe or to appraise their experience in the light of experiences by others. To the fundamentalist, this openness is at least the first and may be the final and fatal step toward letting truth and meaning get bartered away and forgotten.

The moderate, the liberal, and the modernist, not unbelievers but other-believers within traditions, somehow appropriate the distinctive revelation or experience, but they do not find it necessary to aspire to a total or even decisive break with what some theologians call "ordinary secular experience." They are more ready to acknowledge the symbol as symbolic and to be aware of the multivocality of symbols. They acknowledge a hermeneutic approach to texts, traditions, and reality, in which they reckon with the standpoint they and their community bring to religious experience and behavior. They may well belong to multiple communities, while fundamentalists tend to concentrate on their own. So one may be a Jew of this denomination or that; of this or that political predilection; of this fraternity or sorority or that; choosing to join this club for one purpose and that voluntary association for another—and in all of them receiving some positive experiences from others who would have been characterized as threatening or evil by fundamentalists.

They are empowered by the call of their faith—we are not here speaking of the nonreligious, though fundamentalists may call them such. But they relate this power to other forms of power: aesthetic, political, social, and ideological, again negotiating their way in selective, if sometimes reflexive, ways. They have a mission born of faith, but it is a mission among others that a free citizen undertakes in open community. While they may not always find it easy to do so and while their ancestors may not have done so, they seek ways to deal with the other in positive and mutually beneficial ways without dealing their own faith and community away to the point of their own destruction.

To fundamentalists, the first signal of compromise or positive regard of the religious other has to be avoided. This does not mean that fundamentalists in many cultures have not learned to be civil in more senses than one, which means both in the *civitas* and in manners. But their acts of interpretation are not allowed to be as generous or risky as these are for those with other styles of religiosity or who are at home in a secularity of their own description and choice.

I assume that a keynote should include some reference to what to do about the world thus described, especially if the movement toward peace instead of violence is favored. Here we can only sketch beginning traces. I would include the following:

- The pluralist—as we will call the believer or nonbeliever who is not a fundamentalist and who is relatively at home in a liberal culture—will find it necessary to listen carefully, portray the fundamentalist accurately, and not "lump together" all people they do not understand into a single fundamentalist camp or category. Such listening will demand at least a minimal expression of respect for the other, not in mere condescension but as part of an effort to understand the stimuli to fundamentalist responses and the reason for fundamentalist worldviews and expressions.

- The pluralist who has listened may well attempt to address some of the addressable features of experience that plausibly occasion fundamentalist response. Where fundamentalisms are attractive to the uncommitted because they are poor, discontented, or disgusted with secular and repressive regimes that are nominally professing their own faith (for example, in Algeria), there has to be some address to social circumstances off which militant fundamentalisms feed. By the time of outbreak, it is very difficult to bring forth concessive and peacemaking gestures from both sides.

- One expects that religious voices inspired to provide alternatives to fundamentalism cannot be noncommittal, semicommitted, or merely tolerant. I like Gabriel Marcel's concept of counter-intolerance, which a fundamentalist will at least understand since he or she might not have any empathy for light tolerance. Instead of saying tolerantly, "I don't believe much of anything and I expect you not to, and then we can live and let live," the counter-intolerant says and shows, "I believe something so deeply that I understand what your belief means to you, and I use the attachment to and comprehension of my belief structure as a warrant, a guarantee, of your own."

- In the years ahead, it will be important for the committed but not intolerant or not militant to show that belief for one's own self and community need not issue in persecution, an impulse to exile or distance "the other," or consistent misunderstanding of them. Secular observers who have read the history of religion and some philosophers, ideologues, and psychologists may point out and then taunt, "If you are anything but fundamentalist or fanatic, you don't really believe." Faith and community may not need God, but they need a devil. Give that up, and you are on a slippery slope toward non-faith and post-community.

- In the face of it, there are good reasons for understanding more of the commitment by the faithfully generous, including some of the recent popes, any number of post-Holocaust Jewish leaders, the Gandhis, Martin Luther Kings, and Dietrich Bonhoeffers, all of them flawed—but all of them capable of retaining commitment and community while rejecting the impulse to demonize the other. They are precursors, running ahead of those who would work in ways to transcend the violence of a violent century with approaches to peace, not in utopia, but in the uncharted temporal territory of a new century.

PART II

---

*The Possibility of Peace in
Judaism, Christianity, and Islam*

RENE-SAMUEL SIRAT

The Roots of Peace in the Torah

The work of righteousness shall be peace,
and the effect of righteousness quietness
and confidence for ever. (Isaiah 32:17)

I t is a harrowing experience for a rabbi, for an ordinary Jew,
to speak at Auschwitz, and to come to speak of justice, peace,
confidence, and serenity. As the French poet Alfred de Vigny put
it, "only silence is great." Long ago, the Psalmist expressed the
same idea magnificently in the following words: "For you, Lord,
only silence is prayer" (Psalm 65:2). This is the verse which I
quoted at Geneva during the meeting between four cardinals and
a delegation of European Jews. I had a private discussion with
Cardinal Franciszek Macharski, and since that day I have had
unshakable ties of friendship and unlimited admiration for his
courage. This quotation came spontaneously to my mind when he
asked, "Why is the Jewish community utterly opposed to the
presence of the Carmelites who pray and perform acts of
penitence?" I was the only rabbi in the Jewish delegation, and out
of all of us he wanted to ask me this question. The emotion with
which I replied, in the face of unspeakable anguish, clearly spoke
for itself and even constituted the deciding factor.

As we were coming back after this private conversation, he
expressed his wish to sign the Zakhor statement with which you
are all familiar. This response was in marked contrast to the
situation a few hours earlier, when the two delegations, Christian
and Jewish, had met in an attempt to draw up a press release

indicating that things had broken down. Cardinal Macharski's initiative saved our meeting from the impasse into which it had run. Today's events allow me to tell him again, in public, of the great respect I have for him, of my friendship and of my wishes for his good health, and, as the biblical expression puts it, life for a hundred and twenty years.

Speaking at Auschwitz is an extremely difficult thing. Why did I agree to take part in these remarkable proceedings of this international meeting? The reason relates to the chronological jubilee, the fifty years that have elapsed since the *Shoah*, and to the fact that we are gradually moving from the time of memory to the time of history. We wish a long life to the survivors who are here with us, and to them I repeat the same wish: a hundred and twenty, surrounded by their nearest and dearest, their children and grandchildren, thereby finding some peace and serenity.

Despite the absolute horror, despite what the Prophet Zechariah calls "the mourning of Hadad-rimmon in the valley of Megiddon" (Zechariah 12:11), which gave rise in Christian texts to that well-known expression for absolute and total horror, we have now survived fifty years after the *Shoah*. It is our duty to ask ourselves a number of questions, questions which revolve around justice, peace, and more generally, around the basic values of which we are the bearers. We are speaking, above all, to the third generation, the generation of the children of those who knew Auschwitz, not directly, but through the accounts of their parents who, despite the barbarism which surrounded them, kept the human ideal very high.

The Bible teaches us: "You shall not abhor an Egyptian, because you were a stranger in his land . . . and the third generation may enter into the assembly of the Lord" (Deuteronomy 23:8). "Strangers" in the country of Egypt, in the period of slavery? That is wrong. We were slaves, persecuted, and abused. Hebrew children were thrown into the Nile. How can the Torah state that we were simply strangers, using the same expression as the one used in Genesis when the revelation is made to Abraham: "Know for certain, Abraham, that your descendants will be strangers in a land that is not theirs?" The Bible wanted specifically to eradicate the feelings of perpetual hatred, the desire for revenge, for gratifying humanity's basest instincts. Can this be done by obscuring the truth? We must remember Primo Levi's terrible cry. Unless we act as ever-vigilant witnesses and the custodians of memory, the *Shoah* might, G-d forbid, once again become a reality.

The Bible talks of strangers in Egypt. Is this tantamount to a reduction in the dramatic, absolute, and basic responsibility of the Egyptians and of Pharaoh? And yet, we must indeed consider that the Egyptians, the Idumeans, all beings created in the image of G-d, are also entitled to our respect. If the first generation may not enter the assembly of the Lord because the pain is too great, the third generation may be full members of the Community of the Just.

Here in Auschwitz, every word is agonizing, but I believe it is my duty to make a triple declaration of peace: peace of the Jewish people with G-d, peace of the Jewish people with itself, and peace of the Jewish people with the nations.

Peace With G-d

It is true that we have been indicting G-d for fifty years. How could we accept that this G-d of love and mercy, who is referred to in practically every chapter and verse of the Bible, could have allowed to happen the absolute, ultimate horror: six million of our brethren murdered, just because they were born Jewish. In order to make sure that I am understood properly, let me quote a well-known text, taken not from Jewish, but from Islamic theology.

It is a well-known fact that there was fierce opposition between Ash'ari and his master Al-Jubba I, representing the school of the Mu'tazilites. Ash'ari, a fervent Mu'tazilite, broke away and became the enemy of this school of thought, which was part of Islam from its beginnings. The Islamic tradition teaches us that the break between Ash'ari and his master came about in the wake of a philosophical sparring match whose arguments I would like to summarize here.

Al-Jubba I taught that the rational meaning of human suffering is the "compensation" that G-d "makes sure his servants do not go astray" and is bound to do everything for the best. Ash'ari then, according to the school's tradition, submitted the following problem to him: "Let us take three brothers; one dies as an adult, obedient to G-d; the second dies as an adult, disobedient; the third dies before the age of reason. What happens to them?" "The first one is rewarded by Paradise," replied Al-Jubba I, "the second is punished by Hell, and the third one is neither rewarded nor punished." Ash'ari retorted, "Very well, and if the third one says to the Lord, 'Why did you let me die a child and not let me live, so I could obey and enter Paradise?' What will the Lord say?" Jubba I replied, "The Lord will say, 'I know that if you had grown up, you would have been disobedient and would have entered Hell; so the best thing for you was to die a child.'" Then Ash'ari objected: "If the second one says, 'O Lord, why did you not let me die a child? I would not have entered Hell,' what will the Lord say?" Al-Jubba I was confounded and Ash'ari turned his back on the Mu'tazilites.

As a Jew, I would ask the question differently. Addressing the first question, I would challenge G-d, saying, "Did the spiritual leaders of the Central European Jewish communities who entered the gas chambers reciting the Shema Israel (Deuteronomy 6:4), encouraging the members of their community and their congregations to do the same, really enjoy the reward that G-d promised his righteous ones?" Is this the way that the righteous are compensated here on earth? Of course, I know that Rabbi Yanai taught that on the human level there is no possible explanation for the serenity of the wicked who die in their beds, surrounded by their nearest and dearest, having made hundreds and thousands of human beings suffer; nor for the sufferings that the righteous suffer when they have persevered in their perfect love for their Creator (Ethics of the Fathers, 4:19).

In a famous text that Jews recite on the ninth of *Av*, we remember the destruction of both Temples, the ten martyrs of the faith, and, in particular, the dreadful martyrdom of one of them. The question bursts out from the depths of human revolt: "Is this the fate of those who have observed the Torah throughout all of their lives? Is this the reward that you promised them, Lord?" And G-d's reply is as follows: "If an inhuman cry similar to this were to be heard again, I will return the whole of Creation to the original state of chaos" (Midrash *Ele Ezkera*). And I, an ordinary

Jew among Jews, would be tempted to say: "Well, Lord, return the whole of Creation to the original state of chaos."

Is life really worth living in the face of so many of these martyrs who have studied the Torah, practiced it, and respected it? Despite the many Righteous Among the Nations who risked their lives to fight against the inhumanity instituted by the Nazis and their Vichy henchmen in France, the Horthy supporters in Hungary, and the quislings in so many other European countries, is this creation really such a success that it can continue to exist?

As for the second question, can the Lord assert, facing his people, face to face (Exodus 33:11; Cf. Numbers 12:8), that the million and a half children who died in the gas chambers were immoral in their attitude and did not deserve to live? Would anyone dare assert such a horrible thing? The little sister of Samuel Pisar—about whom he spoke in such moving terms when he gave testimony at the Papon trial—the little girl who went to the gas chamber grasping the hand of her mother, who suffered the same fate, and with her other hand clutching her beloved doll, did she have to be punished? Is there really any human justification for these appalling sufferings? No, of course not.

And the third question, that of Jews who had assimilated and given up practicing Judaism, did they deserve to die in such a horrible fashion? Does the faithfulness of practically all of the Jewish people not constitute an utterly sufficient reason for them to receive forgiveness for their faults committed? Is it conceivable that all these Jews had to die simply because they had to atone for their sins? Is this not the very opposite of what the Torah teaches us?

On the human level, there is no answer to these three questions. But the Talmud has given us something extremely profound to think about (Babylonian Talmud, *Tractate Berakhot*, 3A). The Talmud says that G-d the Holy One, Blessed be He, laments the destruction of His people and of the Temple which is the place of prayer for all humanity.

After fifty years, a feeling of compassion for G-d must dwell within our hearts. I know that what I am saying here in Auschwitz may appear sacrilegious. But I believe with all my conviction that for the Jewish people, this place is actually a sign of the greatest quality of faith and love for G-d by his people, even if we continue to be bruised and weep for those who are no longer with us, and are devastated to the very depths of our being by the *Shoah*, which will remain a pervasive presence in Jewish history until the end of time, or rather, until the coming of the Messiah of justice and mercy.

The Indispensable Reconciliation Between Brothers

The Midrashic commentary on the Song of Songs highlights the difficulty of peace existing between brothers in the first verse of Chapter 8, where it says, "Who can make you a brother for me?" The Midrash (*Midrash Rabba*) asks which brothers are we talking about: Cain and Abel? We know how utterly tragic their confrontation was. Perhaps Isaac and Ishmael? Unfortunately, brotherly feelings were and are not currently the order of the day. I hope they soon will be. What about Esau and Jacob? From the moment of their conception, even before they were called into existence, they fought within their mother's womb. Joseph and his brothers? The reprehensible behavior of the latter is known to all.

We must wait, the rabbis say, for Moses. He was entrusted with the wonderful mission of having to announce redemption to the people, while Aaron, his older brother, had to remain among his people to suffer with them and to bring them courage and hope. It is a wonder that Aaron had not been chosen. But G-d said to him, "Here is Aaron the Levite coming to meet you, and he will see you and be glad in his heart" (Exodus 4:14). The rabbis comment that only G-d can attest that a human being is glad in his heart, because somebody may show all the signs of friendship, affection, and love without, however, these feelings being genuine.

It is a fact that for the last fifty years, since the establishment of the State of Israel, which had been absent from the stage of history for the previous nineteen centuries, we have witnessed an exacerbation of the divisions within the Israeli people and the Jewish people. Whether in the Knesset, Israel's parliament, or outside the Knesset, or in the media, brotherly dialogue no longer exists. We see nothing but one insult after another where people are waiting to use words to attack the person speaking. This is verbal violence which can lead to physical violence. Israel's Prime

Minister was assassinated because for months and months there had been a crescendo of verbal violence against him. Those who ease their consciences today by denying any participation in the crime would do well to examine their consciences over and over again.

There are even divisions between religious and non-religious circles. To hear rabbis speaking with such contempt, such hatred for non-religious people, and to hear Shulamit Aloni express all of her negative opinions about the religious circles in Israel is disgraceful. Additionally, there are increasing divisions between Diaspora Jews and Israeli Jews, or those separating Jews from the various Sephardi or Ashkenazi groups—all those gaping differences which were dictated by the dramatic circumstances of Israel's peregrinations in exile. All of this is distressing and could easily drive one to despair.

"Democracy," said Churchill, "is the worst form of government except all those other forms that have been tried from time to time." The excesses of this system can be harmful when, in the name of democracy, we tolerate various attitudes which are totally opposed to the most basic moral standards. Of course, it is not democracy as such that I am challenging, but its abuse. In the social systems prevailing in the western democracies, everything is based on the party system. By definition, a political party's immediate effect is to divide the electorate, the community, the people. People try to propagandize in an attempt to convince other citizens and thereby achieve a majority vote and hence obtain power, whether on a local, regional, or national level. If this legitimate desire to defend the interests of the party prevails over all other considerations, if there is no longer a national consensus, and if a certain number of values are not indisputably shared by all members of the community, society, and nation, then the nation itself is in danger.

This is why it is important from here in Auschwitz—where Israel's enemies instigated their dreadful scheme to destroy our people, where they made no distinction between religious and non-religious, between those originating from one group and those from another, from one country or another—to return to the ultimate bedrock on which peoples, nations, and societies are grounded. In other words, we must redefine, underscore, and praise to the heavens those elements which constitute a national consensus, which are the values which must prevail, and upon which party-based divisions can have no influence.

It is important for the rabbis to rediscover their real vocation, which is, like that of Moses our teacher, to seek out the lost sheep and bring them back to the flock (*Midrash Rabba* on Exodus 3:1), and not express abhorrence, rejection, or biting criticism of those who do not belong to the same religious group as oneself. There is also a need to take care of one's own problems before getting involved in other people's. We must recover and clearly state the positive values which constitute the bedrock of the people of Israel's continuity and endurance.

Peace of the Jewish People with the Nations

Lastly, it is important for the Jewish people to be reconciled with the nations of the world. Immediately after the *Shoah* this undertaking was, of course, impossible. And yet, visionaries such as Jules Isaac in France, Chief Rabbi Kaplan, and Chief Rabbi Saffran, the current Chief Rabbi of Geneva, and a few others, saw that it was essential to lay the foundations of a Jewish-Christian friendship, which has now borne fruit—very important fruit. The friendship between Jews and Christians is now a fundamental value for all those who reflect about interfaith dialogue.

Pope John Paul II's last declaration about the *Shoah* clearly demonstrates the path that has been walked since the beginning of this century when Theodore Herzl, the visionary and founder of the Jewish state, met with Pope Pius X. Indeed, it is possible to measure precisely this extraordinary journey that has begun between Jews and Catholics. And that which holds for relations between Jews and Catholics applies equally to relations between Jews and Protestants. Friendly relations are also gradually being established between Jewry and the Orthodox Christian world. We must not forget that the largest Jewish communities to have survived the *Shoah* and the Gulag are in daily contact with Orthodox Christian communities, whether in Moscow, the Ukraine or in many other places.

What I would dearly love to see come about and what I have tried to promote as an idea for more than twenty years is a Jewish-Muslim friendship. I have had the honor of meeting with Muslim dignitaries of the highest levels who all agree that this is an opportune moment for brotherly dialogue between Jews and Muslims, following the example of the Jewish-Christian dialogue. It is obvious that this interfaith dialogue must be based on the absolute respect that we owe to each other. It is obvious that we must dismiss from our approaches any idea of syncretization or proselytizing. Then, after making peace with G-d and with our Jewish brethren, we will have made peace with all of brothers and sisters who are also created in the image of G-d. Tempered by the vision of the Valley of Tears of the Gehenna endured here on earth (Psalms 84:8), we will all be able to hope that death will be overcome and, in the words of the prophet, "G-d will wipe away the tears from every face and will swallow up death for ever" (Isaiah 25:8). It is this aspiration that I wish to express here today.

War has made too many victims. It must be outlawed. There is no such thing as a holy war in Christianity, nor in Islam, nor in Judaism. Only peace is holy, for peace is the name of G-d (*Midrash Rabba* on Leviticus, Par. 9:9). Only the beautiful word of *shalom*, peace, *salam* constitutes the greeting through which, when brothers meet, they call out divine blessings. *Shalom* is the name of G-d. *Salam* is one of the ninety-nine names of Allah. We hope that, as the great Egyptian President Anwar El Sadat said, there will be no more war, but instead a peace without bounds. This peace was announced by the Prophet Isaiah (Isaiah 11:9), and will cover the entire earth, as a river flows over everything as it passes (Isaiah 66:12), covering the thirsty land and the miseries which came before it (Isaiah 44:3); bringing the living waters (Zechariah 14:8), the waters of joy (Isaiah 51:10-11), the waters of gladness (Isaiah 12:3), and the waters which enable life to be passed on (Isaiah 55:1).

The Jewish people recently celebrated the festival of Passover, and I shall let Primo Levi speak the concluding words. In one of his most moving poems, from *A une heure incertaine*, the hero, whose sense of what is human was further magnified by his incredible sufferings, asks the question confronting our generation:

Passover

Tell me: how does this evening differ from other
    evenings?
How, tell me, does this Passover differ from other
    Passovers?
Light the lamp, open wide the door so that there
    can enter
Gentile or Jew, the pilgrim: perhaps
Under the rags is concealed the prophet.
Enter and take your place among us,
Listen and drink, sing and make Passover.
Eat the bread of affliction
The lamb, the sweet clay, the bitter herb,
Today is the evening of differences,
When we lean our elbows on the table,
Because the forbidden becomes the permitted,
So that evil translates into good.
We shall spend the night recounting what
    happened
Far away, overflowing with miracles,
And through the wine too much drunk, we will
    see mountains
Clashing like rams,
The wicked, the wise, the simple, and the child
This evening exchange questions,
And time reverses its course,
Today flows back into yesterday,
As a blocked river flows back at the mouth.
Each of us was a slave in Egypt,
Has been soaked with sweat and straw and clay,
Has crossed the Red Sea dryshod.
You too, stranger.
This year in fear and shame,
Next year in justice and virtue.

CAHAL BRENDAN CARDINAL DALY

The Roots of Peace in the New Testament

I confess that I find it difficult to speak. How can one speak? What can one say after Auschwitz and Birkenau? Some have said, "Can we speak of God, after Auschwitz?" "Can there be good and evil?" Others have said after Auschwitz, "Can we go on living?" And yet, we must speak of the things that we have seen and heard. We must speak. For people of faith there must be hope. For people of faith, Auschwitz and Birkenau can be that valley of bones of which Ezekiel spoke, where the spirit of God can create out of skeletons, a new life and new hope for a new Israel of God, a new Islam, a new humanity. It is in hope of that hope, as Paul of Tarsus said, "against all human hope" that we have come to this place.

In 1981, I visited the Yad Vashem Museum in Jerusalem, and last year I visited the Holocaust Museum in Washington. I felt overpowered by the horror, the desolation of those experiences—the most harrowing I have ever had until today. The sheer horror of Auschwitz permeates one's whole being. One feels contaminated by the stench of evil. I felt myself swept by a feeling of revulsion against the Nazis, and also of shame and fear for the human race and for myself as part of that human race; shame at what evil we have done, fear for what evils we are capable of performing. And I reflected not how evil they were, but how evil human beings can be, and therefore, how evil I potentially am, because I am part of that same humanity.

Elie Wiesel said, "Not every victim of the Holocaust was a Jew, but every Jew was a victim." I think it can also be said that every human being is implicated in the evil of the Holocaust.

Many of the people who participated, directly or indirectly, in the horror of the *Shoah* were ordinary, respectable people, often good family men, loving husbands and parents, good neighbors living in nice houses—what we would now call a good quality of life.

Many in the wider community and even in the world community who suspected that something terrible was going on, did not want to know. They were not particularly different from us. Who is here among us who does not feel the need to say, "There but for the grace of God go I?"

As a Catholic, I am glad to say that few Christian leaders have gone farther than Pope John Paul II in accepting the full Catholic share of guilt for the Holocaust, or in expressing abhorrence for that unspeakable crime. He has called it a "new paganism," the deification of the nation. Recalling the fiftieth anniversary of the uprising in the Jewish ghetto in Warsaw, he spoke of the crimes against God and humanity and the construction of an insane ideology that was able to set in motion an entire system of contempt and hatred against other human beings, crushing them to pieces. But he also went on to speak of that deep and mysterious union in love and faith with the Jewish people, which he says is experienced by the Catholic Church and by himself—a union which belongs to God's plan for salvation and for eternal reconciliation.

Commitment to that goal of love and faith must be made and implemented by Jews and Christians, separately and together. In April 1994, Pope John Paul II said:

> Christians and Jews together have a great deal to offer to a world struggling to distinguish good from evil, a world called by the Creator to defend and protect life, and yet so vulnerable to voices that propagate values bringing death and destruction. As Christians and Jews, following the example of the faith of Abraham, we are called to be a blessing for the world and it is, therefore, necessary for us, Christians and Jews, to be first a blessing to one another.

This blessing will effectively occur if we are united in the face of the values that are still threatening us: indifference, prejudice, and displays of anti-Semitism.

A critical theme to which the Pope has frequently returned is that of the "common spiritual heritage linking Christians and Jews"—the phrase is taken from the Vatican Council's 1965 Declaration, *Nostra Aetate.* In 1990, addressing the American Jewish community, the Pope said, "The origin of that common spiritual heritage is found in the face of Abraham, Isaac, and Jacob." Within that common heritage we may include veneration of the Holy Scriptures, confession of one living God, love of neighbor, a prophetic witness to justice and peace, and confident expectation of the coming of God's kingdom. As a result, we can effectively work together in promoting the dignity of every human person and in safeguarding human rights, especially religious freedom.

We must also be united in fighting all forms of racial, ethnic, or religious discrimination and hatred, including anti-Semitism. "I am pleased to note," said the Pope, "the significant level of cooperation that has been achieved already over the past quarter of a century, and it is my hope that these efforts will continue and will increase." In 1986, the Pope said, "Jews and Christians are the trustees and the witnesses of an ethic marked by the Ten Commandments and the observance of which man finds his truth and his freedom." To promote a common reflection and collaboration on this point is one of the great duties of the hour. In that common reflection, we must join with the other sons and daughters of Abraham, those of Islam. Those who organized this conference might well have had that program in mind when planning this historic conference.

Pope John Paul II constantly reminds Catholics of our relationship with those whom he calls "our elder brothers in the faith of Abraham." We are a long way from the "perfidious Jews" of the old invocation and the Good Friday Liturgy, which Pope John XXIII struck out of that Liturgy. At Mass, using the first Eucharistic prayer, we speak of the sacrifice of our father, Abraham, the sacrifice of Abel, and the sacrifice offered by Melchizedek, High Priest of God. When we pray the Psalms, we are using the same book of prayers as Jesus and his mother Mary used; as the Jewish people have used down through the centuries and continue to use today. Today, in union with my Jewish brothers, standing in front of the three pillars of stone at the crematorium in Birkenau, I was praying *de profundis*—"Out of the depths, Lord, we cry to you." Quite possibly the very same prayers were being said by my Jewish brothers and sisters.

Pope John Paul II also firmly rejects the idea that it was a matter of incidental, cultural fact that Jesus was born a Jew. On the contrary, he insists that the Jewishness of Jesus is part of the divine plan of salvation and part of our faith. Unfortunately, there is a unique degree of scandal about Catholic anti-Semitism, given the very special bonds that bind us with the chosen people of Israel, and given the patrimony which we Catholics have received from them and share with them. The English Cardinal Manning early this century said to a group of Jews, "I could not understand my own religion if I did not have reverence for yours." I could not understand our sacred writings unless I also tried to understand those we share with you—the Torah. And the two are very closely linked.

The Second Vatican Council in its *Constitution on Divine Revelation* states, "God, the inspirer and the author of both Testaments, wisely arranged that the New Testament be hidden in the Old, and the Old be manifested in the New." It is not possible to adequately understand the Christian Gospels without knowledge of the Torah. And the Old Testament, the Torah, has always been firmly held by the Christian Church to be the Word of God for all times, no less valid and no less necessary for salvation in the Christian era than in the times before Christ. It is true that attempts have been made throughout history to exclude the Torah from the canon of Christian scripture, but Catholic and Protestant churches have firmly rejected such impulses. One of the saddest images that I retain from my visit to the Washington, D.C., museum is the sight of the desecrated and half-burned scrolls of the Torah from the days of the infamous *Kristallnacht*. And I felt as revolted by that scene as a Jew would be, for the Torah is my sacred scripture, too.

In a celebrated series of Advent sermons preached in St. Michael's, Munich, in 1933, Cardinal Folhaber spoke of the Nazi attempt to outlaw the Jewish Bible and so-called Jewish morality, in the name of German Christianity. He retorted, "To eliminate so-called Jewish morality would be to eliminate much of Christian morality, too. Christ, after all, regarded the Decalogue as the basis of his own moral teaching, and he held it to be binding on Gentiles as well as on Jews." Cardinal Folhaber devoted another one of his sermons in Munich to the ethical values of the Old Testament and showed how they are reaffirmed and supported in the Gospels. In still another sermon, he spoke of the social values of the Torah and their relevance for Christians.

With all of this theological and sacramental reflection, we now turn to the roots of peace in the New Testament. The New Testament understanding of peace carries all the rich resonances of the Hebrew *shalom*. It includes, of course, the meaning of the absence of war and violence, and much more. *Shalom* means the fullness of spiritual, mental, and physical well-being; proper relationships between man and woman and God; between man and woman in marriage; between a married couple and God; and respect for God's plan for human flourishing, and all of creation. As a greeting, may I say that the Hebrew *shalom* and the Christian *peace* have similarities with the blessings familiar to ancient Irish spirituality, *Beannacht J De'Oraibh*, "The blessing of God be with you." God be with you is the origin of the English phrase, "Goodbye" or "God by you," now being replaced by the trivial "bye-bye."

New Testament peace, like *shalom*, is much more than a human condition with a merely horizontal dimension. It has an inseparable vertical dimension which comes down from God. Peace is God's gift, and is not merely the result of our unaided making. Peace depends on right relations with God. When these relations have been violated by sin, peace demands their reparation by the repentant seeking of God's forgiveness.

Jesus distinguishes between the peace as humans commonly understand it and the peace that he has won for us. "Peace I leave with you, my own peace I give to you. Not as the world gives, do I give to you" (John 14:27). The peace that Jesus gives is the peace that he has achieved by his death on the cross, accepted voluntarily by him as a sacrifice of atonement for human sins. This is a sacrifice that we recall and make sacramentally present in our Eucharist, where we have the body given up and the blood shed for us and for all so that sins may be forgiven.

In preparation for and celebration of the receiving of that victim, Catholics try to fulfill two conditions: First, we call to mind our sins and ask forgiveness from God and from one another. Second, we exchange a sign of peace with our neighbor. We are asked at that moment to think also of the neighbor whom we have wronged, or who has wronged us, and to form the prayer that all may be well between them and God and between them and ourselves. Such are some of the rich meanings of Christian peace, which incorporate the beauty and the richness of the Hebrew *shalom*, especially when we place peace in the presence of Christ himself, who is our peace.

Peace is one of the dominant themes of the New Testament. The word peace occurs ninety-two times in the Christian scriptures and is found in almost every book of the New Testament. As noted above, it has a vertical and horizontal dimension. Where the vertical and the horizontal meet is a cross, and the cross on which Jesus died is a fundamental element in the New Testament's understanding of peace.

The reconciling death of Jesus on Calvary is *the* root of peace in the New Testament, and especially in the writings of Paul of Tarsus. We find it most fully developed in his letter to the Ephesians, where he asserts that Christ is our peace and has broken down the barriers that used to keep us apart. Jesus did this to create a single, new man in himself and unite them both by restoring peace through the cross. In his own person Christ killed the hostility. I link this with the strange words that Paul uses elsewhere about Jesus: "He who knew no sin was made sin for our sake." I feel that I have gained new insight into the meaning of that strange phrase, especially from my visits to museums in Jerusalem, Washington, and the valley of death, which is Auschwitz and Birkenau.

Jesus, for Christians, is God-made-man. For many non-Christians, Jesus is one of history's great religious leaders, someone of exceptional religious insight and sensibility. Jesus took all human-made evil upon himself, all human sinfulness, and shuddered at the awfulness, the filthiness, the corruption, and the stench of it, and freely accepted his own death as an atoning sacrifice to his Heavenly Father. This was so that sinfulness might be redeemed, that humanity might once again be put at peace with God. Once established, this primary peace between humanity and God gives the promise to believers of a peace between individuals and peoples where a divided humanity can become a single, united new humanity.

To reiterate, in his own person Jesus killed the hostility. The hostility that Paul is primarily talking about in this context is the hostility in the Christian communities of his own time, between Christians of Jewish background and Christians of Gentile background. And he seems, at a quick reading, to ascribe that hostility to the rules and decrees of the law. Is that not introducing a new source of hostility? A more careful reading of the text reveals that Paul is criticizing the law only when or if it is used to set up barriers within the Church between Jewish Christians and Gentile Christians; e.g., making the dietary and ritual prescriptions imposed on Gentile Christians a factor for division and confrontation. But Paul is not condemning the law. Does not he say about his brothers of Israel, his own flesh and blood, that they were adopted as sons, they were given the glory and the covenants, they were given the law and the ritual, and the promises were made to them? They are descended from the patriarchs, and from their flesh and blood came Christ, who is above all, God forever blessed. As the Chosen People, he goes on, they are still loved by God, loved for the sake of their ancestors. God never takes back his gifts and never revokes his choices. In his own person Jesus killed the hostility.

How is it then that this very death of Jesus seems in the Gospel to be blamed on the Jewish people, who thus seem to be branded as a guilty people, an accursed people? How is it that these very Gospels, with their message of peace, could become a route not of peace, but of that very anti-Jewishness which has marked much of the Christian era? There are a few things that can be said, or need to be said in response to these questions. First of all, the so-called cursing of the Jewish people is a misreading of the Gospel account itself, because Jesus himself acquits the Jews of blame. He says, "Father forgive them, they do not know what they are doing." In the Acts of the Apostles, Peter, addressing the Jews in Jerusalem near to the Temple, says to them, "I know that neither you nor your leaders had any idea what you were really doing."

The Roman soldiers are depicted in the Gospels in a much worse light, treating Jesus cruelly. The "guilt" of the Jews in this Gospel context is not the guilt of killing Jesus, but the guilt of not believing in him. The whole context in which the passion of Jesus is set by the Gospel writers is a Jewish one—a Jewish cultural and religious context. Clearly, the writers had in mind passages like Jeremiah 26, where the prophet speaks to all the people of the town of Judah who came to worship in the temple of the Lord, and he warns them in the name of the Lord, "If you will not listen to me, I will treat this temple as I treated Shiloh and make this city a curse for all the nations of the earth." And he went on to say to them that if they did repent and listen to the words of the Lord, the Lord would spare them. "But," he declared, "if you do put me to death, you will bring innocent blood on yourselves, on this city and on its citizens."

A similar picture is found in the Book of Wisdom and in the Songs of the Servant of the Lord in Isaiah 42, 49, 50 and 52-53—the four songs of the Servant of the Lord. The descriptions of the sufferings of Jesus in the Gospels are obviously influenced by the accounts of the sufferings of the Just One in these purely Jewish contexts. They do not, as such, have an originally anti-Jewish connotation. In fact, Josephus regards the destruction of Jerusalem by the armies of Titus as being God's punishment for the impieties, murders, and outrages committed in Jerusalem.

Finally, we have to say that Christians living in the Hellenistic and Roman culture and the post-Apostolic generations read the Passion narratives in the light of the Judeo-Christian versus Gentile-Christian divisions in their own time, and misread the Gospels as justifying their own anti-Jewish prejudices. In still later centuries the Gospels were read as a literal history—as we understand history today—with no understanding of how sacred history was written in the biblical milieu of Jesus and his immediate disciples, the authors of the first oral and written Christian traditions. In fact, I suggest, the tragic and shameful story of Christian anti-Semitism is in part a story of how people with hostile attitudes towards other nations or other races always seem to manage to find in their own sacred writings religious reasons for their own racist prejudices, scandals, and so-called holy wars. The conclusion which Christians should draw must be to repeat what Pope John Paul II has said, "Anti-Semitism, never again, never again anti-Semitism."

The cross for Christians was intended to be a sign of reconciliation reflected in the establishment of peace on earth among all people. It was a perversion of the Christian under-standing of the cross when the Crusaders used it as a badge for a so-called Christian crusade against Islamic, Jewish, and other enemies instead of what it authentically represents for Christians: a sign of forgiveness, a sign of love of enemies, a sign of reconciliation.

Two instances of reconciliation, in particular, I want to select from the ministry of Jesus: that of Jews with Gentiles and that of Jews with Samaritans. On many occasions Jesus speaks of Gentiles as people of faith, generosity, goodness, and openness, and thereby he is seeking to change negative attitudes about Gentiles into positive ones, and hopes to foster reconciliation between the two.

Second, the quarrel between Samaritans and Jews was acute at the time of Jesus. It was an ancient quarrel, going back at least to the refusal of the Samaritans to assist in the rebuilding of the Temple in Jerusalem after the Assyrian conquest, and to the building of an alternate Samaritan temple. Feelings of hostility ran high. In one passage Saint John writes that some angry Jews could find no worse term, no more abusive term to hurl at Jesus than "Samaritan." They cried, "You are no better than a Samaritan!" And John dryly remarks, "Jews do not associate with Samaritans."

We are also told in Luke's Gospel that Jesus and the disciples, coming down from Galilee for the great Jewish feasts in Jerusalem, sometimes found it too dangerous to pass through Samaria. They made their way, instead, along the borders and took the longer route down the Jordan Valley and then went up from Jerusalem to Jericho. It is all the more striking that Jesus should locate his parable of the Good Samaritan on that very same Jericho road, contrasting the charity of the hostile and hated Samaritan with the heartlessness of the most pious of Jews—the Priest and the Levite. In fact, in the Gospels, Jesus never once uses the term Samaritan, except as a term of praise. He loves the Samaritans as people of virtue, holding them up as models to imitate. He changes the language of relationship between the two peoples. The hated Samaritan, symbol of contempt, becomes instead the Good Samaritan, symbol of charity and virtue.

Conversion of the language of communication between peoples is an important condition of change in relationships between them. If words can dehumanize, demonize, and kill, then words can also evoke love and encourage reconciliation. And that surely is what Pope John Paul II is all about when he speaks of "our elder brothers in the faith of Abraham," instead of "unbelieving Jews." If we seriously set about to change the names we use about others, the jokes we tell, and the songs we sing, then we will have taken an important step towards changing relationships between peoples. Jesus says:

> Love your enemies. You have heard how it was said, "You must love your neighbor, hate your enemy," but I say this to you, "Love your enemies, pray for those who persecute you and, in that way, you will be sons and daughters of your Father in Heaven, for he causes the sun to rise on the bad as well as good, and his rain to fall on the honest and dishonest alike."

Notice that even in this passage Jesus is quoting that it had been said that one must hate the enemy. Unfortunately, these words have been mistakenly held to be a caricature of the teachings of the Torah. But Jesus praises the Law, he declares that he came not to condemn the Law, but to fulfill the Law. What he is referring to is surely passages in the prophets, pronounced on enemies, so-called "cursing psalms," and so on; but not the Law, as such. Love of enemies already taught in the Law is strongly emphasized in Jesus' teaching about peace. And Jesus, like Paul after him, speaks of the time of the Messiah, the Messianic time, as a time of peace when "the mountain shall bring forth peace for the peoples, and the hills, justice. In his days justice shall flourish and peace until the moon fails" (Psalm 70).

Indeed, we seem far from that blessed time. The fields of ashes over which we walked today, the valley of the shadow of death in

Auschwitz and Birkenau, these show how debased the human heart can become, how opposed are its ways to the will and the way of God. But Christian faith, like Jewish faith, has looked for the blessings of peace, not just the human efforts—though these are important—but above all, the Blessed One's loving kindness, mercy, and faithfulness.

Anne Frank, in May 1944, wrote in her diary, "What, oh what is the use of war? Why can't people live together peacefully? Why are people so crazy?" In July 1944 she wrote:

> I simply can't build my hopes on the foundation consisting of confusion and misery and death. I've seen the world being gradually turned into a wilderness. I hear the distant thunder, I hear the approaching thunder. It will destroy us, too. I can feel the sufferings of millions and, yet, if I look up into the heavens, I think it will all come out right in the end, and that cruelty too will end and peace and tranquillity will return again.

Anne does not use explicitly religious language here, but I doubt that she would have written like that, or thought like that, but for the echo in her of that Jewish faith that sustained her ancestors in the many and long tribulations of their history and kept hope alive for many, even in Auschwitz and Birkenau and Buchenwald and all the concentration camps of Gentile shame. I find in Anne's words echoes of a psalm beloved by Christians, which we owe to you, our elder brothers and sisters in the faith of Abraham:

> I lift up my eyes to the mountains from where shall come my help. My help shall come from the Lord who made heaven and earth. May he never allow you to stumble, let him sleep not, your God. No, he sleeps not, nor slumbers, Israel's God. The Lord is your God and your shade; at your right hand he stands. By day the sun shall not smite you, nor the moon by night. The Lord will guard you from evil, he will guard your soul; the Lord will guard your going and your coming, both now and forever. (Psalm 121)

A MIRA S HAMMA A BDIN

The Roots of Peace in the Qur'an

P eace be upon you and God's mercy and his blessings. This is
the obligatory form of greeting in Islam.

I shall outline the fundamental principles that govern the
issues of peace and violence in the Qur'an, and explore the laws
and rules that govern them. I shall then give examples of how the
Prophet Muhammad, peace be upon him, applied the Qur'anic
rules in practice when he established the first Islamic polity in
Medina, because the Sunna—the reported sayings and deeds of the
Prophet Muhammad—is second only to the Qur'an. Thus, it is
obligatory on Muslims to follow it because Islam is not only a
theology, it is also the framework of a sociopolitical identity.

The Qur'an is believed to be, literally, the Word of God.
Hence, the Word was made Book. The Qur'an in Islamic thought
is comparable to Jesus in the Christian tradition, in the sense that
both are perceived as the central revelations of God. The position of
the Sunna could be compared to the Bible's position in Christianity.

The Qur'an is neither a book of legal codes, nor a systematic
theology, nor a book on ethical morality *per se*. The Qur'an is a
book of faith from which we should derive laws, ethics, and the
theology we need in order to define the type of human society
that God wants us to be, and from which we are able to define
the ethical theology which would help to explain the meaning and
purpose of this life. To deduce laws from the Qur'an, we must
look at its entire message. We must seek out the values that form
the general objective of Qur'anic legislation and injunctions.

The Qur'an begins the story of creation by telling us that God
created humans as distinct and superior to all other creations

(38:71-2, cf. 2:34, 15:29, 20:116). God created all humans as equals, from one soul, one entity (4:1, 31:28). He bestowed on them dignity (17:70), and decreed the human soul to be sacred (5:32), with no difference between a Muslim and a non-Muslim soul: "He who slays a soul unjustly, it is as if he has slain all of humanity" (5:32, 6:151, 17:33, 18:74, 25:68).

God made humans his vicegerents (2:30, 6:165, 27:62, 35:39) so that they could do his work on earth. He made them superior to all other creations by the fact that he bestowed on them the power of reason and gave them the freedom of choice (33:72). Because humans could choose between right and wrong, and good and evil, the Qur'an tells us that God sent every community an apostle with guidance (16:36, 22:67, 2:139). This apostle always delivered the same primordial message, that of surrender to the one and only God, who said to the Prophet Muhammad in the Qur'an, "Nothing is said to thee other than which was said to all the messengers that preceded thee" (41:43). Muslims are enjoined to respect and revere all these apostles and not differentiate between them (2:136, 285, 4:151, 42:13).

In the Arabic language the word for surrender is *islam*, which comes from the root SLM, from which also comes the word *salam*, which means peace. Hence, the name of the religion Islam combines the meanings of surrender to God and peace. All the prophets who came before Muhammad were Muslims in the sense that they surrendered to God, not that they were followers of the Prophet.

God has ordained that there be different religious communities on earth (49:13, 30:22), and that they must all respect one another (49:11). Discrimination is forbidden on any basis, including religion, because it is God's will that there be different religions on earth until the last day. The Qur'an reads,

> Unto every one of you we have appointed a different law
> [*Shari'a*] and way of life. And if God had so willed it, He
> would have made you all one single community, but He
> willed otherwise, in order to test you by means of what
> He has given you. So vie with one another in doing good
> deeds, unto Him you shall all return, and then He will make
> you understand all that on which you have differed. (5:48)

Freedom of religious belief is absolute in the Qur'an, which states, "There shall be no coercion in matters of faith" (2:256), and "The truth is from thy Lord, let him who wills, believe in it, and let him who wills, reject it" (18:29, cf. 107:6). Freedom of religion is also stressed in verse 10:99: "If it had been thy Lord's will, all who are on earth would have believed. Will you then compel people against their will to believe?"

God also tells the Prophet that interaction between religious communities should be marked by kindness and discussion, not violence when he says: "And argue with them in the most kindly manner" (16:125). To the Muslims the Qur'an says, "Do not argue with the People of the Book except in the most kindly manner, and tell them, 'We believe in the message that has been revealed to us and the messages that have been revealed to you and our God and your God is one and the same and we are all surrenderers, Muslimeen unto Him'" (29:46, cf. 3:64, 41:34, 9:129).

To be a Muslim one has to believe in the One and only God, his prophets and their books, the angels, and the Last Day of Judgment. A Muslim must believe in the brotherhood of humans which must be protected by the moral values of equality, justice, and honest and fair dealings as ordered in the Qur'an—even between enemies or those one dislikes (42:15, 4:58, 135). The Qur'an reads:

> O believers, be ever steadfast in your devotion to God, bearing witness to the truth in all equity; and never let hatred or enmity of any people lead you into the sin of deviating from justice. Be just, this is the closest to being God-conscious. (5:8)

However, the most important of all Islamic concepts with regard to pluralism and peace is the issue of exclusive salvation. Religious particularism and exclusivism are two of the main reasons for intolerance and violence. The Qur'an is very clear on these issues. God refutes the idea of salvation exclusivity in the following verses:

> Surely, those who have faith in this divine writ, as well as those who follow the Jewish faith, and the Christians and

the Sabians, all who believe in God and the Last Day and do righteous deeds shall have their reward with their Lord, and no fear need they have, and neither shall they grieve (2:62, cf. 5:65).

The logic behind the above verse is fundamental to the belief that God is just. "The Just" is one of the most important of the ninety-nine names or attributes of God stated in the Qur'an. Hence, because God is just, he sent his guidance to every community on earth, each in its own language or way of life. Thus, God has sent them all a true guidance, which would ultimately give them the chance to attain salvation as these two verses indicate: "They have the Torah containing God's injunctions . . . wherein there is guidance and light" (5:43-44), and "Let then, the followers of the Gospel judge in accordance with what God has revealed therein" (5:47).

If God had given only Jews or Christians or Muslims the right message, then he would have acted unjustly by purposefully misleading all the other millions of people. But since God must be just, then all the messages have to be legitimate for the adherents. Otherwise, heaven would be a very empty place indeed, particularly if we consider the various factions within each religion who claim to be the only correct interpreters and true adherents, and as such, the only legitimate claimants of salvation and exclusive residents of Heaven.

The Qur'an states unequivocally that all humans are decreed equal on earth and in the hereafter. The only difference between them, in the eyes of God, is their consciousness and awareness of him and the good deeds they do. If God decrees that all humans are equal, how can we—believing religious humans—decide otherwise?

This notion of equality within pluralism should not pose a threat to one's own beliefs and absolute truths. Believing in one's absolute truths does not mean that one shows disrespect for the other's absolute truths. In my experience, the more I understood about the truths of others, the clearer my own truths became and the more I understood my own beliefs. Yet, at the same time, I became more critical about the concept of absolute truth. I think that sometimes it is necessary to instill some healthy skepticism in our certainty of absolute truths, just as it is important to try to find a rational basis within our certainty for the sake of a deeper understanding of each other.

Turning now to the application of the above principles of equality to the concepts of peace and war in Islam, it is important to say that Islam is not a completely pacifist religion. The Qur'an orders Muslims to fight and to sacrifice their lives and wealth in *jihad*, a word which many of you have heard, and which is incorrectly interpreted as "holy war." The word *jihad* comes from the root JHD which means to exert effort, to strive and to struggle. There are fourteen levels of *jihad*. The highest level and the "greatest *jihad*" is the exertion of effort against one's own evil or sinful inclinations. The next eleven levels are all directed towards peaceful exertion of effort against the ills of society for the sake of promoting truth, fairness, equality, and so on, using such peaceful methods as the *jihad* of the tongue and the pen. The "smallest *jihad*" as it is legally defined, is the *jihad* with the sword. However, whenever the Qur'an mentions *jihad* with the sword, war and fighting against unbelievers, it is always understood in the strict context of defense against aggression and violence. The first verse in the Qur'an to permit fighting and the use of violence says:

> Permission to fight is given to those against whom war is being wrongfully waged—and verily God has indeed the power to give them victory. Those who have been driven out from their homelands against all right, for no other reason than their saying, "Our Lord is God." If God had not enabled people to defend themselves against one another, then all monasteries and churches and synagogues and mosques—in all of which God's name is abundantly extolled—all of them would have been destroyed. And God will support those who support Him. (22:39-40)

Therefore, the *jihad* of violence is permitted in defense of freedom of belief and in defense of one's homeland when it is threatened, and against aggression of those who "observe towards the believers, neither pact nor honor. It is they who are the transgressors. . . . They break their pledges after making a treaty with you and assail your religion" (9:10-12). The following verse continues, "Will you not fight a folk who broke their solemn pledges and proposed to drive out the Prophet and did attack you first?" (9:13). Another verse also says, "And wage war on all the idolaters as they are waging war against all of you" (9:36).

The above verses are all from Chapter 9 in the Qur'an. There are 114 chapters in the Qur'an called *Suras*. Each chapter begins with the words, "In the name of God the most Gracious the most Merciful." This sentence is obligatory when one starts to read any chapter of the Qur'an, except for Chapter 9 in which it is omitted, because this chapter deals with the issues of war and violence. By removing his name from the beginning of the chapter, God makes it very clear that he is against war and violence, even though war is sometimes necessary. All the verses that talk about war and fighting in the Qur'an are constrained and restricted to defensive purposes only. Expansionist *jihad* is not cited or allowed in the Qur'an. *Jihad* should be limited to defensive purposes only. It is important to note that Muslims have not always observed this condition of defensive *jihad*.

On the other hand, the Qur'an also orders Muslims to make peace whenever possible: "And if they incline to peace, incline thou also to it, and trust in God" (8:61). Here God is telling Muslims not to be afraid of peace and to put their trust in him whenever peace is possible, because "He knows what they do not know" (2:30, 2:232, 2:366, 16:74), which is a major concept in Islamic belief. Another verse says, "If they let you be, and do not make war against you and offer you peace, then God does not allow you to harm them" (4:90). Another verse says, "And know that God invites humanity to the abode of peace" (10:25).

The Qur'an goes even further than just making peace. It says that it may even occur that God will ordain love between enemies because God is all-powerful, all-forgiving and all-merciful. God lays down the basis of peace and violence very clearly when he says:

As for those of the unbelievers who do not fight against you on account of your faith, and neither do they drive you out of your homelands, God does not forbid you to show them kindness and to behave towards them with full equity, for verily, God loves those who act equitably. God only forbids you to turn in friendship towards those who fight against you because of your faith, and drive you out of your homelands or aid others in driving you out of your homelands, and it is those from among you who turn towards them in friendship, it is they who are truly the wrongdoers. (60:7-9)

The above verses define clearly and unequivocally the specific defensive conditions under which violence is permitted for Muslims. These verses also clarify that an equitable and just peace is highly recommended. However, dealing with texts is always problematic, in the sense that people with religious commitments may choose to believe that the truth is exclusively an eternal or pre-existing reality, that is, a reality beyond history. But people are also involved in the process of interpreting truth. Anyone approaching a religious text brings with him or her the indispensable baggage of race, class, gender, and personal history. This baggage influences and colors the way that individuals approach the text. The challenge to readers is to avoid a selective literalism where some people might choose or lift those verses that merely suit their purposes, prejudices or, most dangerously, their violent political agendas.

Selective literalism is a favorite practice of extremists on the one hand and those with secular tendencies in all religions, on the other. For example, extremist Muslims might read, "Fight the unbelievers," and stop. They omit the rest of the sentence which says, "as they fight you." Unfortunately, they frequently apply this method to all of the fighting verses in order to legitimate their violence.

Another example of selective literalism is found when some Muslims justify drinking alcohol and gambling by quoting a verse which says, "They ask you about alcohol and gambling," then they skip the next sentence, "In both there is great evil," and proceed to the next line, "They have some benefit for humans" (2:219). So the argument becomes, it is lawful to drink alcohol and to gamble because God says these things benefit humans. This pattern of selective reading is dangerous. There is a verse which says, "Do not attempt to pray while you are in a state of drunkenness" (4:43). It would be interesting to note the interpretation if one stopped reading after "do not attempt to pray." I believe that a responsible interpretation of any text should be one that takes into account the full understanding of the underlying unity of the text and the totality and essence of its message.

Examining the personal history of the Prophet, the *Suras* attest to the fact that he only fought for defensive reasons against the unbelievers who were plotting or fighting against him, his message and his people. When he was told that the Byzantines had gathered a large army to attack him at the northern borders of the Arabian Peninsula in a place called Tabuk, he also gathered a large army and went there. After camping there for two weeks, the Byzantines pulled back without attacking and the Prophet went back to Medina without fighting them. He could have attacked but he did not. Some of the Muslims were very angry because they believed they would have won the battle, and they asked the Prophet why he chose not to attack. He quoted from the Qur'an, "And fight in God's cause those who wage war against you, but do not commit aggression, for verily God does not love transgressors" (2:190). It was on this occasion that the famous verse of *jizya* was revealed. The verse reads:

> Fight against those from among the People of the Book who do not truly believe in God, nor the Last Day of Judgment, and do not consider forbidden that which God and His Apostle has forbidden, and do not follow the religion of truth—which God has enjoined upon them— until they pay the exemption tax [*jizya*] with a willing hand, after having been humbled in war. (9:29)

This verse was directed against the Byzantines who were oppressors of the Christians and the Jews of the Middle East. It specifies a certain group of the People of the Book, namely those who did not believe in God or the Last Day. These are not the same people described in the verse cited earlier: "The Jews and the

Christians, all who believe in God and the Last Day and do righteous deeds, shall have their reward with their Lord, and no fear need they have, and neither shall they grieve" (2:62, 5:69).

It should be noted here that the verse of the *jizya* has been lifted out of context from the underlying unity of the Qur'an to suit the sociopolitical situation of the time. In those periods it was universally applied to all Christians and Jews in the Islamic Empire, partly because Islam was assumed to be a nationality as well as a religion. Those who did not belong to this religious nationality were resident protected people, but second-class citizens. As such, they were not allowed to fight with the Muslim army and had to pay the *jizya*, which was the war exemption tax. Also, in most historical periods they were not permitted to hold sensitive positions in the state. It is interesting to note that today in Israel, where the Jewish religious identity decides the nationality of its citizens, the Palestinian Muslims and Christians who hold Israeli passports and who are supposedly citizens of the State of Israel are not allowed to enroll or fight in the Israeli army and are not permitted to hold sensitive positions in the state and are practically treated as second-class citizens.

Modernist Muslims are arguing now for the true interpretation of this verse and for the end to the concept of *jizya* in Islamic law, since it is discriminatory and not applicable in the modern nation state, except for Israel, where the allegiance is to the state and not to the religion. It is imperative that such laws are actually changed in writing and not merely argued about. As long as these laws remain on paper somewhere, they remain a tool for people to misuse or manipulate for their own purposes.

The Prophet was the first person to put the Islamic pluralistic and peaceful ethos into practice. When he established the first Islamic polity in Medina, he drew up what came to be known as the Constitution of Medina. In this document, the Jews of Medina were declared to be "one community with the believers, [where] they have their religion and the Muslims have theirs" (n. 25). The Constitution of Medina also says:

> Each must help the other against anyone who attacks the people of this document. They must seek mutual advice

and consultation, and loyalty is a protection against treachery. . . .

To the Jews who follow us belongs help and equality. They shall not be wronged nor shall their enemies be aided. . . . The Jews must contribute to the cost of war by bearing their own expenses just like the Muslims. Everyone shall have his portion of the spoils, from the side to which he belongs. (nn. 37, 45)

The pluralistic terms of this document remained valid with many Jewish tribes except with those tribes who sided with the enemies and plotted against the Muslims. Jews remained in Medina until six years after the Prophet died, when the Third Khalifa Omar exiled them from the northern peninsula. However, they have remained in and around Yemen until this day. In fact, when the Prophet died, his shield was pawned to a Jewish man in Medina.

In many periods in Islamic history, the sociopolitical situation has prevented the possibility of applying the pluralistic and peaceful ethos of Islam. However, putting this Islamic ethos of pluralism and peaceful coexistence into practice is possible and feasible, particularly since there are many examples in Islamic history where this peaceful ethos was practiced successfully, such as the period of the Golden Age in Spain. The concept of pluralism and living in peace with the "other" is so fundamental to Islam that God has interwoven it into the most sacred of Islamic institutions, the nuclear family. The family is so important in Islam that most of the legal injunctions in the Qur'an deal with family matters. Muslims are permitted to marry non-Muslims, loving them as wives and husbands and accepting them as parents of their offspring. Muslims are also allowed to eat the food of non-Muslims and to befriend them as in-laws, relatives, and friends (5:5).

I believe that the most important task that faces us as reasonable, responsible, religious people is the task of challenging the uncritical and self-interested interpretation of religious texts which should be based on the fullness of the religious message, while bearing in mind the overriding principles and objectives of the legislation and other injunctions. Religious people must be careful not to indulge in selective literalism when they are dealing with their texts. Otherwise, they might risk falling into the trap of misguided interpretations, as is the case with hard-line extremists and those who use religion as an excuse or an umbrella for violence and for their political agendas.

Most important, I believe that we should change the misinterpreted laws in writing, so that they are not there to be misused, and so that logical and reasonable interpretations can reach the lay people—most of whom are moderate and form the majority of any religion. It is only then that we can affect real change towards true pluralism, respect, and peace. Maybe then, as Dr. Marty suggested, we can enhance the part of religion that heals and minimize the part which kills.

PART III

Bridges to Greater Understanding

DAVID ROSEN

The Role of Religion
in the Pursuit of Peace

Religion has often been criticized, especially in modern society, for having been a source of war and conflict rather than a vehicle of peace. In support of this contention, such critics not only point to bloody medieval religious wars, but also to modern conflicts as far apart as Northern Ireland and Sri Lanka.

Apologists for religion claim that such clashes as these are not religious conflicts but rather territorial conflicts in which religion is used as a weapon. They state further, as did Cardinal Maria Martini at a recent interfaith conference in Assisi, that "such manifestations in the name of religion are nothing less than a distortion and perversion of religion"; i.e., they are not part of true religious expression. I personally share Cardinal Martini's contention and thus conclude that despite our denominational and doctrinal differences, our perceptions of both the essence and purpose of religion are very similar. However, there is the rub. Both he and I have colleagues who do not see the essence and purpose of their religions in this same light, and many who see their religions as justifying and encouraging hostility towards others. Accordingly, I wish to delve further into the character of this problem and draw constructive insights for the role of religion as a force for peace.

Religion, in essence, seeks to give meaning and direction to the place and purpose of our existence in the world and is thus bound up within the circles of human interaction from the smallest, such as family, to the broadest, humanity, or even creation as a whole. These circles make up our identity as individuals and also as social beings. From family through congregations, communities, ethnic groups, nations, peoples of faith, to international frameworks, these circles are the building blocks of our multifaceted identities, and we ignore these components at our peril. Indeed, modern ethnologists and popular social anthropologists have attributed much of modern disorientation and alienation to the breakdown of traditional society and these building blocks, especially of family and community. Alvin Toffler, for example, in his book *Future Shock*, highlighted the problem of mass deracination in modern society and the serious destabilizing consequences of such rootlessness. He and others like Robert Ardrey have explained the proliferation of religious sects and cults as well as the drug culture and other such phenomena in modern society as the search for meaning and identity amid a void resulting from the breakdown of traditional societies and the concomitant vacuity and loss of identity.

In this inextricable relationship between religion and identity, religion gives meaning and purpose to our understanding of who we are as part of smaller units or circles that broaden to make up the wider circles and greatest whole. However, in affirming who we are as part of those smaller circles, we also at the same time declare who we are not. Accordingly, the components of our corporate identities may be used not only for positive affirmation but also for negative division and conflict, whether these be between families, communities, or ethnic or national groups. Religion is inextricably bound up with the different components of our identities. Where these identities are expressed negatively, religion becomes part and parcel of such conflicts, exacerbating hostility instead of defusing it, as we see in so many parts of our world today.

However, precisely because religion addresses not only the smallest component of identity but also the broadest, religion has the very capacity to counteract conflict and exploitation of differences, by emphasizing those dimensions of human commonality that should bind people together above and beyond the particular, different components of our identities. A high degree of security and stability is required in the smaller circle in order for the wider circle to be able to relate positively to it.

In his work, Robert Ardrey draws on zoological parallels and points out that paradoxically, when there is an absence of security or a threat to one's security, this condition serves as an effective stimulus to build identity and social solidarity; e.g., societies in times of conflict. Accordingly, religion acquires far greater prominence in times of insecurity, precisely as a vehicle for nurturing the particular identity that is threatened or undermined. In such conditions of threat and insecurity, René Girard points out, societies develop the need to identify an object of blame—a scapegoat, which religion facilitates in its own special way. Moreover, in a situation of direct conflict, the opponent is usually demonized in order to strengthen a sense of justification of one's identity, position, and claim. Sometimes such needs even breed an astounding obsessive compulsion to present the scapegoat, or perceived threat, or even real threat, as the totality of evil. The historian Richard Hofstadter describes this presentation of the other as the image of "a perfect model of malice." In such a context, religion as a vehicle of comfort and security, in the face of a real or perceived threat to the particular identity concerned, is likely to be so caught up in this role that its function becomes limited to introspection, reflecting the insecurity of the particular group involved. All too often in such a context, it becomes a vehicle for the pursuit of xenophobia and bigotry and betrays its metier, alienating itself from the wider circles of the universal human identity.

As indicated above, in order to be able to move beyond the smaller circles of our identities, we need to feel secure in relation to any wider circles of commonality. Such security is not only a matter of material needs but also of a profound psychological nature, relating both to the perception of the wider circle and to the way the person or group feels that they are perceived within the wider circle.

Implicit in these thoughts is a central thesis about the relationship between the particular and the universal. As mentioned, particular components of our identities are so fundamental to our inner being and psycho-spiritual welfare that only a universalism that emerges out of our particularisms has any hope of contributing to peaceful coexistence. A universalism that does not respect these particularisms is not only of a dubious moral character that manifests itself in cultural imperialism and triumphalism, but it is ultimately unsustainable and evanescent because it is without real roots and stability. On the other hand, particularism that is without universal aspiration and sensibility is ultimately narcissistic and idolatrous, betraying the vision of religion for a better world for all.

At times there will be individuals of remarkable stature who will rise above the rest. As a rule, they are representatives of institutional religion who reflect rather than lead their communities and are unable to apply themselves to relations between and beyond their communities if they feel threatened, whether by political or socioeconomic conditions. In fact, for precisely these reasons institutional religion itself is unlikely to be the vehicle for the resolution of such conditions. However, when breakthrough does take place and these conditions improve, then religion may and should play a crucial role in providing the psycho-spiritual glue necessary for securing the processes of development and peace, as in the case of the Middle East today. In order to do so, however, the need for security must not be underestimated. A positive attitude towards the wider circles of which we all are a part requires that we feel secure in our inner circles in relation to the former. I refer not only to security from military threat, physical violence, and economic threat, but also to security from the threat of disrespect and vilification.

If our religions are to be a force for peace in our relations with each other in this time of political breakthrough, then we must explicitly teach respect for each other. Essential for true respect is a degree of modesty. Our religions teach that arrogance is tantamount to idolatry—to the worship of self. While each of us believes his or her particular religion to be truthful, the presumption that truth is exclusively contained only in one's own particular religion is religious arrogance, limiting the divine relationship with humankind. Indeed, it should be easiest for us—all the children of Abraham, the sibling religions of ethical monotheism—to be able to appreciate the divine value within each other's tradition. If we have not done so, it is either because the burden of history and negative experiences weighs heavily on our shoulders bending us over so that we do not stand up straight and look each other in the eye truthfully and faithfully; or it is because religious arrogance blinds our sight.

True respect means that we strive to see and understand others as they see and understand themselves, but it also implies our willingness for self-criticism. In this regard, I recall the first public Jewish-Christian-Muslim trialogue in which I participated in Rome in 1990. I remember listening to an eminent colleague who preceded me as the Jewish speaker at the first session on the subject of religion and peace. He presented an encyclopedic array of Jewish sources extolling and advocating peace and then launched an attack on Christianity for all the horrors that have been committed in its name. Similarly, he warned of the dangers posed by the growing political influence of extremist Islamic fundamentalism.

As I listened to him I recalled the famous passage in the work, the *Kuzari*, by the eleventh-century Spanish Jewish poet and thinker, Rabbi Yehudah Halevi. Halevi relates a story of the conversion to Judaism of the Khazar people, led by their king in the region of the Crimea in the eighth century. The book is entitled *An Apology for a Despised People*, and thus reflects the historical and cultural setting in which Jewry found itself, notwithstanding the fact that Spain at that time provided the most desirable context available for Jewish life to flourish. The book consists of a dialogue between a Jewish scholar and the King of the Khazars.

On two occasions, however, the scholar has no answer for the King and acknowledges the fact. The one occasion is when the King says to him, "You tell me of your love for the land of Israel, of how it is the heart of all lands for you and that only there can the Jewish people fulfill its identity and purpose. Then what are you doing here? You should be there." And the scholar acknowledges that he has no adequate answer in reply. (In fact, Tradition claims that Yehuda Halevi himself did leave for the land of Israel only to be trampled to death by a soldier on horseback.) But it is the other occasion when the scholar is at a loss for a response of which I was reminded at that colloquium. This is when the scholar deprecates Christianity and Islam saying, "They say one thing but do another. They may speak of peace but they oppress and persecute and subjugate others. But we Jews do not do that!" "Of course not," the King retorts, "You do not have the power to do it. Who says you would have been different if you would have had the power?"

As easy as it is to criticize others, it is more difficult to criticize oneself, even to the limited degree of saying, "There but for the grace of God go I." A willingness to recognize that as human communities we are not perfect and the desire to improve ourselves accordingly is extremely important if we are to avoid the blindness of religious arrogance. Indeed, there are few areas that demonstrate the genuineness of commitment to religio-ethical improvement as much as our attitude towards those who are different from us. In this regard, I would make mention of another great Spanish Jew—arguably the greatest of them all—Moses Maimonides, who lived a few generations after Halevi and who succinctly expresses Jewish teaching on this subject.

In his *Code of Jewish Practice*, the *Yad Hahazakah*, in the section on the Laws of Kings, chapter 10, paragraph 11, we find the following passage:

> Our sages commanded us to visit the sick even of heathens and to bury their dead with the dead of Israel and to provide for their poor amidst the poor of Israel for the sake of "the ways of peace," for behold it is stated, "and his mercies are extended to *all* his creatures" (Psalm 145:9), and it is stated, "Torah's ways are pleasant ways and all her paths are peace" (Proverbs 3:17).

This text, including the latter quotation is taken from the Talmud (*Tractate Gittin* 59B), where it also states, "The whole Torah [i.e., the whole of Judaism] is for the sake of the ways of peace." Accordingly, the citation "all her paths are peace" is clear. Even if not stated explicitly in the Torah, there are deeds and actions that nevertheless constitute Torah-true conduct—conduct that is in true consonance with the teleology and purpose of Torah and the revealed Divine Will. That is conduct that promotes peace in the world.

Even more illuminating is Maimonides' own introduction of the quotation from Psalm 145:9. Why does Maimonides refer to the Divine Character, when he is concerned with codifying human conduct towards others? Evidently, Maimonides is referring here to the sublime Torah teachings of *imitatio Dei* (Leviticus 19:1) "to cleave to the Lord" (Deuteronomy 10:20), and "to walk in his ways" (Deuteronomy 13:5). Jewish tradition understands the latter to mean emulating, to the extent of our human ability, the divine attributes of mercy, loving-kindness, truthfulness and forgiveness (cf. Exodus 34:6). In the words of Abba Shaul, "Just as he is gracious and compassionate, so you be gracious and compassionate" (*Mekhilta*, Canticles 3). Similarly, the Babylonian Talmud says:

> Just as the Lord clothes the naked as he did with Adam and Eve, so you clothe the naked. Just as the Lord visited the sick, as he did with Abraham, so you visit the sick. Just as the Lord comforts the bereaved, as he did with Isaac, so you comfort the bereaved. Just as the Lord buries the dead, as he did with Moses, so you bury the dead. (*Tractate Sotah* 14a)

Accordingly, Maimonides is reminding us that just as God's compassion extends to all his creatures, so we must emulate such compassion to all, especially (as the Torah itself emphasizes) toward the vulnerable: not only the vulnerable of our own community—the poor, the orphan and the widow—but also, and in particular, the stranger, the other. Precisely, this principle and such practice demonstrating respect and responsibility towards the other are described in Jewish Tradition as "the ways of peace." In other words, if we really care about peace, we will behave with respect and compassion to all human beings, regardless of their race or creed.

In this new era, in the Middle East and the Mediterranean as a whole, religion has a crucial role to play in promoting such respect and responsibility towards others, based on the profound religio-ethical teachings which we share. But the challenge will only be met if our religions teach respect towards others, not just on the basis of the universal principle of our common humanity, but also out of recognition and respect for our different particularities. Such teaching and conduct will afford us all the sense of security that, together with improved political and economic conditions, will enable our communities to relate effectively and positively to each other in the years ahead.

When we thus rise above fear and insecurity to avoid the pitfalls of scapegoating, stereotyping, and demonizing, and open our communities to embrace the Divine Spirit that is reflected in the life of the other, then we will live up to the noblest vision of our Abrahamic tradition. For Abraham, "God's friend," is mandated to be "a blessing" to all humankind. Our Jewish sages tell us that the greatest of all blessings is that of peace, declaring that "God only created the world so that there would be peace among all" (Numbers, *Rabbah* 12:1).

Pastoral Reflections

It is a great honor to be part of this program and to respond to the invitation that came from Rabbi Ehrenkranz. I would like to speak not as a scholar but as a pastor from a Roman Catholic perspective, about three points: 1) religious inspiration for movements of peace; 2) the spiritual significance of the year 2000; and 3) recent signs of bridges being built.

First, there are movements toward peace coming out of the religious community. This is particularly connected with what Pope John Paul II has done. I think of his first trip to Poland, where there was an unprecedented electricity in the air that happened because a Slav pope had returned to his own land. An enthusiasm and energy was generated that made it possible for the word "solidarity," uttered by him in Polish, to take on a spirit that transformed a people.

A friend of mine who was from Slovakia, living in the United States, said that with the first visit of the Pope to Poland there was a small change. But in two or three years, the people who were afraid now had the courage they needed to practice their faith—directly linked to what Pope John Paul II had done and set in motion in his visit to his homeland.

In January of 1998, the Pope also went to Cuba. Everyone is saying that the entire country was influenced by his visit. It was the first time that they have been able to celebrate Christmas in many years. It was the first time that Cuban television showed images of Pope John Paul II and broadcast his letter—a special message to Cubans which said that he cared. It had an electrifying effect, I was told, even on people who had no belief. They saw that someone from outside was interested in their well-being and was coming to spend some time with them.

He came and the enthusiastic crowds were enormous; they were moved and changed. I knew something else was happening because the bishops had been invited for a meal with Fidel Castro. Castro had been deeply impressed by his meeting the year before with the pope and now he wanted to also work with the bishops.

The effects of the papal visit were felt not only in Cuba, but also in Miami, where some in the Cuban population are now advocating lifting the sanctions against that land. Clearly, attitudes are changing. I believe a movement that began with religious preaching has made the difference that will pave the way for democracy and peaceful change, we pray, just as was the case in Eastern and Central Europe.

Rabbi Rosen spoke of the importance of not losing our religious identity. I agree with him very much on this. There is something else that must not be lost, namely, hope. Some bishops from the United States met with representatives of the Church in Latin America and we talked about the problems of our poor in the great cities. Those of us from the United States noticed a difference between the poor in our inner cities and the poor in places like Rio and São Paulo. The main difference was that our poor seemed to have no hope. I think the reason for this lack of hope is linked with a loss of identity, as well as confusion about culture which results in many kinds of curious and violent behavior.

I also believe that we need to work to restore religion and a sense of hope, direction, and peace-making with many of our young people. Again the pope has been a catalyst in restoring hope and faith. Whether it was World Youth Day in Denver, with its hundreds of thousands, or in Manila with five million, or in Paris last August where 750,000 young people from all around the world came out to be challenged, the pope encouraged young people to go back to their roots of faith, truth, love, self-denial, and prayer, in order to exercise their free choice in making a world where there can be trust and peace among all people. That is one way in which I see a preacher of faith helping us today recover hope and work for peace.

Imam W. Deen Mohammed, who has been a dear friend since his visit with me in Baltimore in 1995, mentioned the spiritual impact that the year 2000 will bring. I would now like to reflect on this.

The charter that Catholics have been given is the document which Pope John Paul, II issued in November of 1994, an apostolic letter entitled *Tertio Millennio Adveniente (On the Threshold of the Third Millennium)*. In fourteen closely-reasoned pages, the pope touches on such issues as the meaning of the millennium and the place of the jubilee in the Hebrew Scriptures, the jubilee in which our Christian jubilee celebration is rooted. The Jewish law specified every seventh year as a sabbatical year and, as recorded in Leviticus 25, every fiftieth year as a jubilee, which was a time for freeing slaves and returning property. Pope John Paul II observes that these goals for the jubilee were ideals seldom realized in practice. But he did point out that the notion of the jubilee found in the Hebrew Scriptures helped to shape the concept of all visible, created riches as serving the common good for all humanity. This is the vision that serves as the basis for our teaching of the principles of social justice and is a basis of building peace.

Before issuing his apostolic letter, the pope convened an extraordinary meeting of the College of Cardinals in Rome in June of 1994. This meeting contributed substantially to several ideas which Pope John Paul II developed in his letter, especially that there should be an examination of conscience, repentance, and the promoting of fitting ecumenical and interfaith initiatives by the Church. "We look back and repent," the pope said, "of the acquiescence given, especially in certain centuries, to intolerance and even to the use of violence in the service of truth." Accordingly, in addresses which he delivered in Prague, he made reference to Jan Huss; in Paris he recalled in the spirit of repentance the St. Bartholomew's Day Massacre; and in Rome he has repeatedly stated repentance for the hurtful impact of Christian anti-Judaism on the Jewish people. In these ways he has been carrying out, and will continue to carry out, the injunction he gave to himself and to our Church: "This jubilee is not to be a time of triumphalism."

People of faith need to consider seriously the present situation in the world as we approach the jubilee. First, we should be more vigilant in countering religious indifference with charity and enthusiasm. Second, there is a loss of the transcendent sense of human life. Life has meaning only in terms of the eternal destiny that God has given us in creation. We are made in God's image and destined to return to God. Third, there is ethical confusion today, even about the values of human life and the family. This confusion is directly related to loss of identity and to the serious collapse of values across the board in society.

As the entire Church prepares for the millennium, Pope John Paul II established a central commission to oversee and coordinate the preparations. In this central commission is a committee devoted specifically to ecumenical and interreligious concerns. It struck me that here is a new and dramatic development. We find a Church of a billion people reaching out and asking for advice from others, so that we can celebrate a great event in our internal life in a way that will be sensitive to others. We are choosing to involve them, embrace them, and to the extent that we can, celebrate common principles of justice and peace to lift them up. I am confident that when the final synod of bishops of the year 2000 is held, the synod will involve all of the continents and it will include a strong interreligious presence, even as there is an interreligious presence in the preparations for the jubilee itself.

This is what Pope John Paul II said about the ecumenical and interreligious aspect of the jubilee: "The eve of the year 2000 will provide a great opportunity, especially in view of the events of recent decades [I think the events he had in mind were the *Shoah*, the emergence of the State of Israel, the collapse of Communism, and the vitality of Islam in the Middle East and in industrialized countries in the Northern Hemisphere] for interreligious dialogue in accordance with the guidelines set down by the Second Vatican Council in its Declaration, *Nostra Aetate* (*On the Relationship of the Church with Non-Christian Religions*)."

Pope John Paul II has stressed that dialogue with Jews and Muslims should have "a preeminent place," and he personally looks forward to joint meetings in places of exceptional symbolic importance, such as Bethlehem, Jerusalem, and Mt. Sinai, so that new facets of our relationships will continue to emerge. Pope John Paul II wants us to lift each other up in prayer as we move forward.

In many communities there is a treasure to be assembled in partnership with art museums or an hour of glory to be achieved through a concert with the help of a symphony orchestra or a great choir. The beauty of art, the power of music, and the eloquence of the written or the spoken word can be instruments of building bridges involving both faith and culture. Those who remember the Holocaust concert at the Vatican in April of 1994 know what a powerful moment that was. It was on that occasion that the Pope voiced some of his strongest statements on the *Shoah* and the need not to forget it. But it was also a moment of enormous impact for people who heard or watched through television, music helping to plumb the depths of the human spirit.

I will now say a word about some recent signs of bridge building that I have seen. So many good things are happening.

First, over the years, our own United States Conference of Bishops has developed pastorals on such issues as the challenge of peace, the United States economy, and Catholic social teaching. We devoted time to listening to what Jewish and Christian scholars, speaking on behalf of various organizations, could tell us. Worth noting is our pastoral letter on the economy, which has strong roots in the teaching of the Hebrew Scriptures. In particular, our pastoral statement, *Toward Peace in the Middle East,* reflected extensive consultation in the United States and in the Middle East with Jewish, Christian, and Muslim leaders. When we finally went to our full body of bishops, we said that we had heard many different voices and we were able to present a statement which has continued to guide our conference ever since, especially when we reflect on the Middle East.

Second, as part of a recent interreligious pilgrimage, I heard of something that had not happened before that was about to take place: a meeting has been planned in Toledo, Spain, of Jewish, Christian, and Muslim leaders from Jerusalem. And I had the impression, listening to the Muslim who told us about it, that they were hopefully looking at peace from the perspective of religion. The man who informed us of the meeting was a political leader, which I thought was a very good sign.

And lastly, here in Poland at the Catholic Eucharistic Congress, I saw a sign which struck me as very special. The first day of the sessions, the day on which Pope John Paul II flew up from Rome, the program included, at the pope's request, an unprecedented service that was both ecumenical and interreligious. Archbishop Jeremiasz, who was with us last night, was a participant in that service and there were many other Orthodox and Protestant Christians in attendance. There were also three rabbis. In his address, Pope John Paul II spoke very strongly of our need to approach the coming great jubilee in humble companionship with each other.

At the end of the service, in the presence of more than 10,000 people and with live television covering the event throughout Poland, the pope embraced each of the major participants. The three rabbis came last. As Pope John Paul II embraced each of them the place exploded in applause. And I thought, the pope has as a title, *Pontifex Maximus*, the "Great Bridge Builder." Here, in an instant of reaching out to embrace each of these people, but now most especially the rabbis, he has built a bridge that words and documents cannot build. He has done it with a sign. It was a sign of something deeper than friendship. It was a sign of deep trust, admiration, and respect for his brothers.

And I believe that these days have been another sign to me. You who are people of faith, openness, and trust have reached out to each other to build bridges. Please God, may they be bridges that will bear a lot of traffic.

GEORGES COTTIER

The Great Jubilee:
A Time of Remembrance

I offer these reflections in order to bring up the theological problems of the Inquisition as they are seen from the viewpoint of the Great Jubilee. At the same time, I will give you the reasons for which the Historical Theological Commission for the Great Jubilee thought it necessary to call on specialists of the historical sciences, who had specifically studied the problems that concern us here.

For the Church, the words and the works of Jesus represent the fulfillment of the tradition of the Jubilee, a heritage of the Old Testament. One is reminded of the episode of the Synagogue of Nazareth related in the Gospel of Saint Luke (4:16-21). Taking the book of the prophet Isaiah (61:1-2), Jesus read this passage: "The Spirit of the Lord is upon me, because he has anointed me to bring good tidings to the afflicted: To bind up the brokenhearted, to proclaim liberty to the captives, and the opening of the prison to those who are bound, to proclaim the year of the Lord's favor."

"The prophet was speaking of the Messiah," comments the Apostolic Letter, *Tertio Millennio Adveniente* (*TMA*). "Today," says Jesus, "this Scripture has been fulfilled in your hearing" (Luke 4:21), indicating that he was himself the Messiah whose arrival had been foreseen and that the long expected "time" was beginning in him. The day of salvation had arrived, in the "fullness of time." Thus, all subsequent Jubilees relate back to this "time" and are concerned with the messianic mission of Christ (see *TMA*, sec. 11).

In the biblical tradition, the Jubilee Year was the year of the reestablishment of equity among the children of Israel based on a double certainty. First, to God alone belongs the *dominium altum* over the goods of the earth, so that all wealth is the common possession of all people. In the image of divine justice, social justice must protect the weak. The second certainty is based on the memory of the liberation from captivity in Egypt that God realized for his people. The Jubilee Year was the year that slaves were set free, for humanity cannot remain forever in a state of slavery.

Year of grace of the Lord, the Jubilee Year is the year of forgiveness of sins and the suffering which comes from them; it is a year of reconciliation between adversaries; it is a year of conversions; and it is a year of forgiveness. One understands, then, that the Great Jubilee, which is extraordinarily important since it marks the two thousandth year since the birth of Christ (whatever the exact chronology), is an opportunity to proclaim great joy. "The Church rejoices in Salvation. She invites everyone to rejoice, and she tries to create conditions to ensure that the power of Salvation may be shared by all." Respecting the rhythm of the times, the Church "intends to walk forward with every individual, bringing each to understanding," so that each period of history "is imbued with the presence of God and with his saving activity. In this spirit, the Church rejoices, gives thanks, asks forgiveness and presents petitions to the Lord of history and of human consciences" (*TMA*, sec. 16).

We should note a final expression: a bond that unites history and conscience. Both history and conscience have the same Lord, and although the conscience is not all-powerful, it is at work in history, whether it be a clear conscience, a troubled one, or a conscience betrayed or gone astray. In short, from a theological standpoint, one cannot eliminate ethics, nor can one eliminate a religious dimension from history. Earlier, we read this astonishingly compact and dense expression: "In Jesus Christ, the Word made flesh, time becomes a dimension of God who is himself eternal" (*TMA*, sec. 10).

If I have thus briefly mentioned what *Tertio Millennio Adveniente* (sec. 9-16) tells us about the Jubilee, it is because we have there the coordinates from which one can understand the religious meaning of seeking forgiveness, about which now we must say a few words:

In the context of the Great Jubilee, we are invited to an act of remembrance, whose novelty, when the Holy Father proposed it, surprised quite a few observers: It is fitting that the Church should make this passage with a clear awareness of what has happened to her during the last ten centuries. She cannot cross the millennium without encouraging her children to purify themselves, through repentance, of past errors and instances of infidelity, inconsistency and slowness to act. Acknowledging the weaknesses of the past is an act of honesty and of courage that helps us strengthen our faith, that alerts us to see the temptations and the difficulties of today and prepares us to meet them. (*TMA*, sec. 33)

Sections 33-36 of *Tertio Millennio Adveniente* specify the sense of this initiative. It is this position which is at the origin of the decision of the Historical Theological Commission to organize a symposium and which conveys the objective that was given to it and the nature of the contribution asked of the participants. But before approaching that last subject, it is fitting to emphasize a certain number of the statements contained in the paragraphs to which we refer and to bring out their theological meaning.

1. The certainty of the forgiveness of God is the basis for all attempts at forgiveness and all requests for forgiveness on our part (*TMA*, sec. 32).

2. For which acts should one ask for forgiveness? A theology of witness contains the answer:

It is appropriate that, as the Second Millennium of Christianity draws to a close, the Church becomes more fully conscious of the sinfulness of her children, recalling all those times in history when they departed from the spirit of Christ and his Gospel and, instead of offering to the world the witness of a life inspired by the values of faith, indulged in ways of thinking and acting which were truly forms of counter-witness and scandal." (*TMA*, sec. 33)

3. We must deal with the theological problem, doubtless the most difficult one, of the relationship between the Church which

is holy, and the sins of her sons and daughters. "Although she is holy because of her incorporation with Christ, the Church does not tire in doing penitence: before God and before man she always acknowledges as her own her sinful sons and daughters" (*TMA*, sec. 33). The central question of the nature of this relationship, which can only be adequately approached in the light of faith, is not the direct object of our discussions here. However, it must be mentioned.

4. After speaking of the sins that are detrimental to the unity willed by God for his people (sec. 34), *Tertio Millennio Adveniente* brings up "another painful chapter of history to which the sons and daughters of the Church must return with a spirit of repentance: the acquiescence given, especially in certain centuries, to intolerance and even the use of violence in the service of truth" (sec. 35).

Now we are at the heart of our theme.

5. It would be in poor taste to remind historians of the dangers of simplifications and partisan readings. However, the Apostolic Letter is addressed to everyone. Consequently, it must deal with images of the past still found in common thought. That is why it is useful to bring up the following considerations of method:

> It is true that an accurate historical judgment cannot prescind from careful study of the cultural conditioning of the times, as a result of which many people may have held in good faith that an authentic witness to the truth could include suppressing the opinions of others or at least paying no attention to them. Many factors frequently converged to create assumptions which justified intolerance and fostered an emotional climate from which only great spirits, truly free and filled with God, were some way able to break free. (*TMA*, sec. 35)

And the text continues:

> Yet the consideration of mitigating factors does not free the Church from the duty to express profound regret for

the weaknesses of so many of her sons and daughters who have sullied her face and have prevented her from fully mirroring the image of her crucified Lord, the supreme example of patient love and of humble meekness. (*TMA*, sec. 35)

It is because its rule is the *sequela* and the *imitatio Christi* that the Church undertakes this reflection, in the certainty that, lead by the Holy Spirit, it will go on in that path. That which was not understood yesterday is today. The Vatican II constitution *Dei Verbum* also writes, "The Church, as centuries pass, moves constantly toward the fullness of divine truth, until the words of God are fulfilled in her" (n. 8).

6. Of the consideration of the past, one must learn lessons for the future: "From these painful moments of the past a lesson can be drawn for the future, leading all Christians to adhere fully to the sublime principle stated by the Council: 'Truth cannot impose itself except by virtue of its own truth, as it wins over the mind with both gentleness and power' "(*TMA*, sec. 35). We have certainly not measured the weight of this statement of Vatican Council II. It is this conviction that today makes possible the seeking of forgiveness. This understanding is of major importance.

7. Finally, we are encouraged to a serious self-examination for the Church of today. "On the threshold of the new millennium, Christians need to place themselves humbly before the Lord and examine themselves on the responsibilities which they too have for the evils of our day" (*TMA*, sec. 36). Let us say that the judgment of the past cannot be disassociated from self-evaluation in the present. They are combined to the extent that the past, for better or worse, weighs on the present. Remembrance, seen from this perspective, is a dimension of the conscience.

For the problems that concern us, the theme of remembrance is central. It interests equally the philosopher and the theologian. It is from that point of view that I suggest several observations.

In speaking of forgiveness and of reconciliation, John Paul II has used the expression "the purification of memory." It certainly does not mean that certain memories must be erased. That would be an impossible requirement. To forget is an act of memory which pushes out painful and traumatizing memories from the field of clear consciousness into the unconscious. What has been thus put away does not stop working. It reminds one of its presence in twisted ways and by cunning disguises; it maintains a latent feeling of guilt until it once again succeeds in bursting out.

To put it another way, memory does not work in an autonomous and totally mechanical way. The subject who remembers is involved in remembrance by his or her choices, fears, dreams, honesty, or cowardice. Remembrance is not neutral, and it is not always innocent. In summary, one can say that it is legitimate to speak of the ethics of memory.

Most significant in this matter is the behavior of Western societies, and above all of their intellectuals, when confronted with the great collective crimes of our century. There exists in this matter an astonishing amnesia, as if these crimes were insignificant mishaps. We know, and yet we do not wish to remember. It is true that the memory of things past is susceptible to the opposite excess. It can become a kind of obsession that suffocates and stifles. We cannot develop here an analysis of the forms of remorse and the forms of guilt. It also happens that the indignant evocation of a distant past can serve as a kind of alibi for the hiding of a more recent past.

The remembrance of the past is itself a part of history, and in that way it becomes an object of the science of history. Historical science studies the images that former generations have successively constructed from an event or reality situated in the past, as well as those metamorphoses and variations of their symbolic weight.

For the understanding of the Church, which was born in that moment of time that Saint Paul calls "the fullness of time" (Galatians 4:4), memory has both a real and specific meaning. The theologian can thus speak of constitutive memory, distinct from a simple empirical memory. I am thinking here of the Eucharist as the memorial of the Lord, where remembrance is the renewal of the present Church through the Pascal Mystery realized once and for all. I am thinking also of the Tradition as a living presence of the Word of God, kept and constantly renewed in its authenticity and vitality, which supposes the grace of the Holy Spirit.

These are mysteries of faith upon which the theologian is called to reflect.

These mysteries constitute the horizon on which one can understand "the purification of memory." John Paul II used this expression during an ecumenical meeting, during which he invited his Protestant and Catholic interlocutors to write together the history of the Reformation "with the objectivity afforded by a profound brotherly charity." The differing judgments of the past continue to maintain divisions. The candid acknowledgment of reciprocal wrongs and errors committed by all sides, "while all had the intention of making the Church more faithful to her Lord," is necessary. "Such a realization," said the Pope in conclusion, "will permit us to hand over the past gladly to the mercy of God, and to be completely free to look to the future in order to make it more closely conform to his will."

I will now underline three statements: 1) charity is the basis in these matters for objectivity of judgment; 2) in order to hand over the past to the mercy of God, we must acknowledge fundamental wrongs and ask for forgiveness; and 3) purification liberates us from the memory of wrongs and ceases to burden the memory as a spiritual trauma, which can paralyze or scar us, as soon as our faults are acknowledged when asking for forgiveness. These statements presuppose a cultural achievement which is at the same time a religious achievement. Historical memory has for its content a body of events, choices, and actions from the past that a social group holds as essential both for its identity and for its destiny. This historical memory is transmitted by generations that maintain it and draw from it their inspiration. In other words, the facts to which one refers have value through their symbolic weight and through their meaning. But it is just as true that in speaking of purification, one recognizes the possibility that intellect and will both have a hold over the meanings of the past; that is to say that they possess the capacity to take back the interpretation of the past. Because the past is always being interpreted, its image requires discernment. The issue of prejudices falls within this area of discernment.

At first glance, the statement mentioned above on the objectivity that comes through deep brotherly charity is surprising. Are we not substituting for partisan partiality something just as negative—the impartiality required by the historian? To this difficulty, one can answer that resentment and hatred, sources of bias and of prejudice, are attitudes that encourage less of the understanding that one expects from a historian than an attitude of sympathy does. Above all, the object on which it focuses justifies this statement, which is of a theological nature. Yet theology, if it is something distinctive, is rooted in a life of faith. The believer who opens his or her mind to the light of the Spirit receives a spontaneous understanding of the Divine. The mind enlightened by the gifts of the Spirit understands as if by instinct what conforms to the plan of God. In its essence, the Church is a communion whose source is the Holy Spirit. That is why the pope can affirm that brotherly charity is the basis of objectivity, because its focus is fully attuned to its object.

However, here an objection will perhaps be raised. What I have just said could lead to a terrible misunderstanding. John Paul II was speaking to Christian historians, both Protestant and Catholic. He did not ask them to stop being historians, as if faith were to replace the real work of historians and the methodological rules that guide them. That would be a fundamentalist approach which would be an offense to the truth. There is something else. In speaking to historians in the context of ecumenism, the pope insisted on the fact that brotherly charity, and not hostility, constitutes the sufficient requisite understanding for the study of the Reformation. It is a question, in other terms, of the spiritual conditions that are most favorable to the exercise of the work of the historian.

Theological reflection needs the work of historians. It cannot, in an excessive vindicatory desire, substitute for that work. In a first phase, the purification of memory consists in endeavoring to give back the past its objectivity by freeing it from the distortions which its image brings. It is up to the historian to try to get closer to the materiality of facts, to establish their causes and their contexts, constantly submitting the results to critical evaluation. Thus, the historian is able to disregard unfounded interpretations and to eliminate myths.

Here theologians can take a page from the book of historians. The *diaconia* of truth to which they strive to be associated with has as its first requirement the respect of epistemological distinctions. A discipline of knowledge cannot, without betraying the truth, be substituted for another. On the contrary, it is by respecting the complementary nature of the disciplines, in which each one is recognized in its autonomy, that we arrive at the truth.

Works Cited

Dignitatis Humanae [*Declaration On Religious Liberty*]. 1964. In *Vatican Council II: The Conciliar and Post-Conciliar Documents*. Ed. Austin Flannery. Wilmington, DE: Scholarly Resources.

Lumen Gentium [*Dogmatic Constitution on the Church*]. 1964. In *Vatican Council II: The Conciliar and Post-Conciliar Documents*. Ed. Austin Flannery. Wilmington, DE: Scholarly Resources.

CONTRIBUTORS

AMIRA SHAMMA ABDIN, Professor of Islamic Culture, Leo Beck College, London

ANTHONY J. CERNERA, President of Sacred Heart University, Fairfield, Connecticut

DAVID L. COPPOLA, Director of Conferences and Publications, Center for Christian-Jewish Understanding of Sacred Heart University, Fairfield, Connecticut

GEORGES COTTIER, O.P., Papal Theologian, Casa Pontificia, Palazzo Apostolico, Vatican City

CAHAL BRENDAN CARDINAL DALY, Archbishop Emeritus of Armagh, Ireland

JOSEPH H. EHRENKRANZ, Co-Founder and Executive Director, Center for Christian-Jewish Understanding of Sacred Heart University, Fairfield, Connecticut

ARCHBISHOP JEREMIASZ, Orthodox Archbishop of Wroclaw and Szczecin, Poland

WILLIAM CARDINAL KEELER, Archbishop of Baltimore, Maryland

FRANCISZEK CARDINAL MACHARSKI, Metropolitan Archbishop of Krakow, Poland

MARTIN E. MARTY, Fairfax M. Cone Distinguished Service Professor, University of Chicago, Illinois

ELISABETH MAXWELL, International Lecturer, London, England

SAMUEL PISAR, Holocaust Survivor, International Attorney, Paris and New York

DAVID ROSEN, Executive Director, Anti-Defamation League, Israel

RENE-SAMUEL SIRAT, Chief Orthodox Rabbi Emeritus of Europe, Paris, France

INDEX